DEATH
AND THE SEXES

DEATH
AND THE SEXES

An Examination of Differential
Longevity, Attitudes, Behaviors,
and Coping Skills

Judith M. Stillion
Western Carolina University

⬤ HEMISPHERE PUBLISHING CORPORATION

Washington   New York   London

DISTRIBUTION OUTSIDE THE UNITED STATES
McGRAW–HILL INTERNATIONAL BOOK COMPANY

Auckland   Bogotá   Guatemala   Hamburg
Johannesburg   Lisbon   London   Madrid   Mexico
Montreal   New Delhi   Panama   Paris   San Juan
São Paulo   Singapore   Sydney   Tokyo   Toronto

DEATH AND THE SEXES: An Examination of Differential Longevity,
Attitudes, Behaviors, and Coping Skills

2 3 4 5 6 7 8 9 0   E B E B   8 9 8 7 6

Library of Congress Cataloging in Publication Data

Stillion, Judith M., date.
  Death and the sexes.

  (Series in death education, aging, and health care)
  Includes bibliographies and index.
  1. Death—Psychological aspects. 2. Sex role.
3. Sex differences (Psychology) 4. Sex differences.
I. Title. II. Series.
BF789.D4S75 1984   155.9'37   84-10801
ISBN 0-89116-313-1
ISSN 0275-3510

To **Glenn, John, Bethany,** and **Daniel,**

whose lives have graced my own

and made it meaningful.

CONTENTS

PREFACE

As I began to write this book several years ago, I realized that to research and interpret a topic as broad as *Death and the Sexes* could be an almost overwhelming task. The time was right, however, to examine in depth the sex differential in death and death-related concerns. After living with this material for so long, I am more convinced than ever that an initial exploration of the topic that attempts to bring relevant data together in one volume is a useful addition to both the literature on sex roles and that of death education.

The book is intended for all people who have an interest in sex differences, sex roles, and/or death-related concerns. However, as is true of all books, it contains the biases of the author. I am currently a teacher of death education and the psychology of sex roles. In addition, I teach adult development and aging. I am also a counselor and have taught courses in group therapy and practiced individual and group counseling. Furthermore, both by training and by inclination, I am a developmentally oriented psychologist. Therefore, this book incorporates an applied life-span focus wherever appropriate. It is my hope that practitioners in various human service fields—education, social work, counseling, nursing, and psychology—may find the material helpful.

Most authors have long lists of acknowledgments included in the preface to their books. I used to wonder why this was necessary, but no longer. Without the help of many people, I could not and would not have written this book. I cannot publicly thank them all. I must, however, acknowledge the most outstanding among them. Hannelore Wass, consulting editor for the Series in Death Education, Aging, and Health Care, invited the volume and gave positive feedback on each chapter as it was completed. Without her initial and continuing enthusiasm, I am sure the book would never have been completed. Two graduate students, Margaret Seaton and Gail Vance, helped to gather material and organize it meaningfully. Colleagues and students who worked on the presentation included in Chapter 3, "Sex Differences in Death and Death-Related Concerns across the Life Span," provided valuable information and served as catalysts for thinking through the outline of the book. To them, Jean Barrineau, Jane Shamblin, and Carol Barrett, I owe a real professional debt. Finally, I wish to acknowledge the help of Faye Inlow and Wanda Ashe, who patiently and cheerfully turned rough drafts into finished products.

Judith M. Stillion

DEATH
AND THE SEXES

OVERVIEW: DEATH AND THE SEXES

Knowledge by suffering entereth,
And life is perfected by death.

Elizabeth Barrett Browning
A Vision of Poets

INTRODUCTION

You are floating in a gray suspended space, only
partially aware of your surroundings. Anxiety begins to
replace the feelings of comfort and security to which
you've become accustomed. The anxiety begins as a pinpoint of disquiet but rapidly becomes more and more
urgent until it reaches a crescendo of fear. Your whole
world seems to begin to change shape. You are caught in
a pulsating contraction of space; squeezed into an ever-
narrowing nightmare. Confusion reigns as you try to
make sense out of what is happening to you; to exert
some control over it.

Finally, in resignation, you surrender to the storm around
you and are pushed by the elements into a narrow tunnel.
You feel closed in, suffocated, claustrophobic. The
pressure becomes unbearable. Just when you feel that
all is lost, you become aware of a light at the end of
the tunnel. With grim determination you hold on and
allow the forces about you to push you toward the light.
In a moment of supreme agony and expectation, you pass
from the tunnel into a light brighter than anything you
have ever imagined. At the same time, you become aware
of a new dimension around you: sights, sounds, smells,
textures which you've never experienced before. You
breathe deeply in ultimate relief and let your breath out
in a sobbing shudder.

Is this a description of a nightmare? Could it be that
it is a description of an experience we all share or will
share? Grof (1) has hypothesized that this experience
may be a partially unconscious recollection in all of us
of the birth process itself. Perhaps you recognize the
above description as having many elements in common with
the "near-death" experiences documented by Moody (2) and
others. Certainly the feeling of compression, the
experience of being drawn through a tunnel, and the
emergence from that tunnel into a world that makes our
past perceptual abilities seem poor indeed are common
elements in the near-death experiences that have received
a great deal of publicity in recent years. Perhaps the
above description characterizes both birth and death
experiences.

It is unlikely that any of us will ever recall the birth
experience well enough to describe it accurately, and
near-death experience accounts can be attributed to
causes other than accurate sensory experiences; for
example, they may well occur as a result of oxygen dep-
rivation to the brain, inducing vivid hallucinatory
experiences. Nevertheless, it is a fact that we have
been observing more rather than less being written about
the accounts of near-death experiences as well as speculation about the lasting effects of the birth experience
on personality. Such interest and speculation by
scientifically oriented people and lay people alike seem
to suggest that human beings have a deep need to know
about the secret mysteries surrounding life. "Where
did I come from and where am I going?" are two questions
that have been asked by human beings since time immemorial.
The presence of the disciplines of religion and philosophy
attests to the need most humans have for answers to these
questions. While both men and women share the need to
explore the unknown that existed before birth and may
continue to exist after death, there is a good deal of
evidence that the space of time between birth and death
is experienced differently by the sexes.

Growth and development throughout the life cycle are
marked by active efforts on the part of all individuals
to structure and understand their world. Growing
individuals bring all of their abilities and identity
to bear in coping with their gradually expanding world.
One of the central cores of the personality around which
much socialization and learning takes place seems to be
gender or sex.

Developmental psychologists tell us that by age 2, we
know whether we are a girl or a boy, although we may not
yet realize that our gender identity is constant. For
example, a 3-year-old, when asked if he is a girl or a
boy, might reply correctly, "A boy." When asked what
he would like to be when he grows up, that same 3-year-

old might very well say, "A mama." Young children recognize their biological sex but don't recognize that it is
unchangeable. By age 5, however, they have learned that
lesson. No "self-respecting" 5-year-old boy would say
that he wants to be a "mama" when he grows up. Indeed,
very few boys until recently would even mention wanting
to be a father as an adult goal. Even more interesting
is the finding that both boys and girls by the time they
enter school can correctly identify stereotypical male
and female activities and attributes and that both sexes
prize more highly those that are recognized as male (3).

It is important to recognize the impact that these early
lessons must have on the developing child. The understanding of gender identity and its accompanying attributes
performs a central organizing function for children. As
they incorporate new understandings in an attempt to
actively master the world, much of what they encounter
is organized around the core of gender. With respect to
the subject of death, questions such as the following
might be raised by the growing child. What does death
mean to a man in contrast to a woman? How should a real
man react to death? Can a man show sorrow, fear, doubt,
anxiety? Are these emotions acceptable for a woman to
display? What are the best ways for a man/woman to cope
with death or threatened loss? Are men and women likely
to experience death in different ways? At different
times? These questions and many more are digested
through the screen of the child's growing understanding
of what it means to be male or female in our society.
The end result of the process may be adult males and
females who exhibit different attitudes, beliefs, and
behaviors when confronted with the topic of death. Let
us briefly examine some of the roots of our current
attitudes toward death as they may color the perceptions
of today's children as they seek to understand the concept of death.

PERSPECTIVES ON DEATH AND THE SEXES

While both men and women have concerned themselves with
the philosophical questions surrounding birth and death,
it is interesting to note that throughout history it has
been women who more frequently have occupied the middle
place between life and death. Perhaps because they
observed women's ability to give birth, early humans
fashioned statues of fertility goddesses and in many
cultures worshiped them. At the same time, however,
they frequently attributed the power of death to women.
Images of "root women" who practice medicine and Voodoo,
and witches who can conjure spells of disease and death
still exist in our folklore today.

A Homeric hymn concerning Mother Earth illustrates the
early Greek idea that both the celebration of life and
the threat of death are lodged in a woman goddess.

> Concerning Earth, the mother of all, shall I
> sing, firm Earth, eldest of gods, that nour-
> ishes all things in the world; all things that
> fare on the sacred land, all things in the sea,
> all flying things, all are fed out of her
> store. Through thee, revered goddess, are
> men happy in their children and fortunate in
> their harvest. Thine it is to give or to take
> life from mortal men. (4)

The message of this early hymn was incorporated in
later Greek and Roman myths in the story of Demeter
(called Ceres by the Romans) and Persephone (called
Proserpina by the Romans). This myth, you may recall,
told the story of a mother, Demeter, whose daughter
Persephone was stolen by the god of the underworld,
Pluto, and taken to live in the land of the dead. Demeter
was so grieved about the loss of her daughter that she
caused a shadow to fall over the earth, and no crops
grew. The entire human species was in danger of starva-
tion. The king of the gods intervened to assure the
future of humankind and made an arrangement whereby
Persephone was returned to her mother for part of each
year. During the time she was with her mother, the myth
maintained, crops grew and people prospered. During the
time she was with Pluto, however, nothing could be
grown (5). This myth is clearly more than an imaginative
story about how the seasons came to be. It is a reiter-
ation of the importance of woman in the whole area of
life and death.

In the Judeo-Christian heritage, we see this theme
repeated in the story of Adam and Eve. You recall that
Eve was the Mother of all living humans, but she was
also the cause of Adam's disobedience. The book of
Genesis says that as punishment for not obeying, the
Lord God said to Adam,

> Because you have listened to the voice of your
> wife, and have eaten of the tree of which I
> commanded you, "You shall not eat of it,"
> cursed is the ground because of you; in toil
> you shall eat of it all the days of your life;
> thorns and thistles it shall bring forth to
> you; and you shall eat the plants of the field.
> In the sweat of your face you shall eat bread
> till you return to the ground for out of it
> were you taken; you are dust; and to dust
> you shall return. (6)

Once again we see that although the woman was the bearer
of life she also brought hardship and death; in this
case, not only to her immediate family but to all generations. The dual message that woman can both bestow the
gifts of life and take them away is still prevalent today.
Perhaps you will recall a recent ad for a brand of
margarine that placed a white-garbed, seemingly benevolent
figure in a lush garden, the personification of fertility.
The ad ended with a loud crash of thunder and the
threatening words from the goddess figure, "It's not nice
to fool Mother Nature."

More recently, the psychological literature of this
century is full of variations on the theme introduced by
Freud that death anxiety is separation anxiety in disguise, and that the separation most to be feared is that
of a dependent child from his or her mother. Freud
believed that awareness of mother absence triggered an
infant's fears that he could not survive independently.
Later situations of loss or loneliness reignited this
anxiety in the developing individual (7). In this way,
followers of Freud maintain that women are the keepers
of the key to mental health, especially when it comes
to issues surrounding the subject of death, as women are
able to lessen death anxiety by the quality of their
mothering, particularly in the early years.

There are also ancient treatments of the relationship
between humans and death that have been passed down into
the present time. In Greek mythology, for example,
Charon was the oarsman who rowed the boat across the
River Styx, from which return was impossible. It is
perhaps this figure that influences people today when
they are asked to draw death. Frequently death is
depicted as an old man with a scythe, cutting down the
living in mid-stride.

The Bible pictures the four horsemen of the Apocalypse--
famine, war, conquest, and death--as male figures. The
dramatic presentation of these horsemen in full gallop
leaves little doubt that violent death especially is
associated with the male of the species.

Early literature, as well as mythology, is full of
heroes who prove their courage by risking death again
and again. The finest reward in mythology, that of
immortality, was reserved for the most heroic of men.
For example, Hercules, after proving himself a dozen
times, was taken to Mount Olympus to live with the gods
as one of them.

And where are our more modern folk heroes like Paul
Bunyan and Pecos Bill? Regardless of the variation in
the folk tale, they are still living and carrying out

their great exploits somewhere in the universe. Such
upbeat endings are rarely seen in tales about women.

It is clear that heroism and death are concurrent themes
for males. The imagery regarding males and death seems
less complex and darkly sinister than that regarding
women and death. Men struggle with each other, natural
forces, and the fates to avoid death and prolong life.
While they have been depicted across the years as more
consistently violent, the violence is overt, often linked
with courage and patriotism, and frequently results in
a reward.

Children incorporate these messages about women, men,
and death into growing understandings of the world. In
addition, they model on the behavior of men and women in
their environment, often learning that death is a subject
adults of both sexes want to avoid. Because of the silence
surrounding the subject, early misconceptions about death
may not be routinely examined and corrected as are misconceptions about less emotional subjects. Children
frequently observe differential reactions from males
and females, as our culture has traditionally approved
more overt grief for females than for males. For example,
children often watch men stoically march off to war and
possible death while women weep. From all these sources,
children in our culture may grow up believing in separate
sex-related behaviors, attitudes, and values regarding
death and death-related concerns.

SEXISM IN DEATH

Largely as a result of the woman's movement in the past
decade and a half, people have begun examining the myths
and stereotypes which both genders have inherited from
past generations, as well as the limitations and dangers
which might accompany these traditional modes of thinking.
During this same period, the emergence of the death
education movement has made available information which
should facilitate this examination in the area of death
and death-related concerns. Three examples of past
differential treatment of the sexes in the area of death
should be enough to remind us that discrimination on the
basis of gender, i.e., sexism, exists in this area as
well as in more publicized areas like salaries and job
opportunities.

We have all heard stories of Greek infants, usually girls,
who were left on a hillside to die. In fact, this
practice has been common enough for one source to state
that "female infants have been considered expendable by
a number of cultures that could not fairly be classified
as 'primitive'" (8). Preference for male children con-

tinues to exist into modern times. A recent study conducted in China, where families are limited to one child
each, indicated that of 99 women who had their fetuses
genetically screened during early pregnancy and were
informed of the sex of their fetus, 30 women elected to
have an abortion. Twenty-nine of the 46 women who were
carrying normal females chose to abort, while only one
out of 53 women carrying normal males made such a choice
(9).

Students of Eastern culture know of the now defunct
practice of suttee, a term that literally means "faithful
wife." According to this custom, outlawed by the British
government in 1829, widows allowed themselves to be burned
to death beside their dead husband on his funeral pyre.
For these women, their lives literally ended when their
husbands died. This practice probably motivated women
to care for their spouses elaborately, but it certainly
did not reflect equal valuing of the lives of females
and males.

A third illustration of sexism in death comes from the
customs of some American Indian tribes, and was popular-
ized in the novel, Centennial (10). In one section of
the book, the author portrays the life of an Arapaho
Indian who is the wife of a great chief. Although she
bore his children and stood by him throughout his lifetime, and although he had accumulated relative wealth
within his tribe, when he died she was left with nothing.
She was considered dead. Her belongings were confiscated
by any tribe member who wanted them. If she continued
living at all, it was only at the sufferance of those
who chose to share their food and belongings with her.
We see traces of this custom reflected in inequitable
inheritance taxes in some states today. One woman who
had worked a lifetime beside her husband to build a
prosperous farm, found upon his death that she was required to pay a prohibitively high inheritance tax. She
lost the farm. Had she died first, her husband would
not have been required to pay any inheritance tax (11).

Continuing evidence of sexism in death-related concerns
has been documented by Kastenbaum (12). He reports the
findings of a study which reviewed death notices and
obituaries in two Eastern newspapers for the month of
March 1973. He found that the distribution of male and
female obituaries in the Boston Globe was 38 male to 13
female and that of the New York Times was similar.
Assuming that the distribution of obituaries should be
similar to the population distribution, he should have
found a 51 to 49 percent balance favoring the females.
Even allowing for the higher male mortality rate which
we shall examine in detail in Chapter 2, the distribution
of obituaries should have been more equitable if both
male and female lives and accomplishments were equally
valued.

In an attempt to determine if the situation had changed
since 1973 and to examine whether the percentages of
male to female obituaries would even out over a longer
period than a month, Stillion and Shamblin carried out
a modified version of Kastenbaum's study (13). Six
months of the year 1977 were chosen at random. All
obituaries published in the New York Times for that
period were reviewed. The results were essentially the
same as those of Kastenbaum. Eighty-three percent of
the obituaries were written about males while 17 percent
were written about females. A content analysis of the
obituaries showed other differences which might be interpreted as reflecting the sex bias of the larger society.
Table 1.1 shows the occupations of the deceased by sex.
Note that the category of the arts was first in the
obituaries of the women while it was fourth in those of
the men. Two categories, those of sports and science,
had no female representation. The professional and
business categories accounted for over a third of the
male obituaries but less than a fourth of the female
obituaries. The category, "Other," which is the largest
for female obituaries, consists largely of people who
rated an obituary by virtue of inherited status or
prominence of relatives including spouses rather than by
personal occupations attainment.

Building on the last point, it is interesting to note
the number of times the spouse was mentioned in each
obituary. The usual custom is to mention the spouse
once. However, in five of the 30 female obituaries in
which the spouse was mentioned, his name was inserted
four or more times. The record number of times for
mentioning a husband was 39. In only one out of 178 male
obituaries that referred to a spouse was the wife mentioned
four or more times. The study seemed to indicate that,

TABLE 1.1 Occupations Mentioned by Sex

Group	Male	Female
Professional	43	2
Politician	28	4
Arts	26	12
Sports	8	-
Military	10	1
Education	26	4
Business	82	11
Writers	26	7
Religion	12	2
Scientists	6	-
Other	3	13

as of 1977, obituaries were still reflecting the lessened value which society as a whole places on the pursuits and accomplishments of women. A recent issue of Omega reports a replication of the original Kastenbaum study utilizing two Rocky Mountain newspapers. In general their findings were supportive of the studies discussed here although weaker in substance. The authors suggest that this may be a result of a history of more egalitarian treatment of women in the western part of this country (14).

In summary, there seems to be ample evidence from myth, historical practices, and current laws and customs that males and females both view and experience death and death-related concerns in different ways. Females tend to be valued less in many cultures. Their status frequently depends on the life of their mates or the whim of their parents or their own physical endurance with little overt support from society.

THE CHANGING PICTURE

In spite of historical and recent evidence of differential treatment of and attitudes toward women in the area of death, American society has been struggling openly to eliminate overt discrimination on the basis of sex from all areas of life. During the past two decades, with the re-emergence of the woman's movement, new emphasis has been placed on the principle of equal opportunity for women to live lives of dignity and worth.

Paralleling the woman's movement, death education as an organized entity has emerged onto the national scene. American people during the first half of this century experienced a dramatic increase in longevity. No longer was death a constant companion. In fact, people born around mid-century could expect to grow to middle adulthood without confronting a death in their immediate family. As a result, it was possible to compartmentalize death, to regard it as something that happened to others or only to the aged. People were aided in their desire to deny death by the fact that medicine was undergoing specialization during that same period. Hospitals were being built in every small town in America, and the family physician who was the source of strength to people from birth through death was being replaced by a series of specialists. Consequently, by mid-century, death had become an action to be accomplished out of sight in a public hospital or nursing home with professionals in attendance. What's more, the topic of death had become one that was not discussed in polite society. As Fulton put it, "death, like a noxious disease, has become a taboo subject in American society and as such it is the object of much avoidance, denial and disguise" (15).

However, beginning with Feifel's book <u>The Meaning of</u>
<u>Death</u> in 1959, the topic of death has slowly become
accepted as one to be examined by serious scholars, practitioners, and the lay public (16).

There is no doubt that today's population is willing and
eager to discuss the varied aspects of death and death-
related concerns. Indeed, a national survey on death
attitudes conducted by <u>Psychology Today</u> in 1970 brought
a greater response than any other survey that magazine
had conducted. Thirty thousand people responded to the
questionnaire. Shneidman, the author of an article
reporting the results, concluded that

> it was almost as though thousands of persons
> had been waiting to unburden themselves about
> death and then felt somehow cleansed after
> writing their unspoken thoughts. Several
> letters said as much, indicating how grateful
> the respondents were and how meaningful the
> exercise had been to them. (17)

For roughly 20 years then, this country has witnessed
two movements coming of age together: the woman's movement and the death education movement. Both movements
have shared two values in common: the belief that all
lives are infinitely valuable and the conviction that
women, as well as men, should have the right and the
responsibility to reach their maximum potential. Further
impetus for individual growth, fostered by death education,
has been created by the realization that the time available for self-fulfillment is limited. The Bragas (18)
expressed this point well when they wrote:

> Death is not an enemy to be conquered or a
> prison to be escaped. It is an integral part
> of our lives that gives meaning to human exist-
> ence. It sets a limit on our time in this life,
> urging us to do something productive with that
> time as long as it is ours to use. When you
> fully understand that each day you awaken
> could be the last you have, you take time
> <u>that day</u> to grow, to become more of who you
> really are, to reach out to other human beings.

A LOOK AHEAD

In light of the values that the woman's movement and
the death education movement have in common, perhaps it
is time for a book which attempts to bring together the
topics of death and the sexes. Men and women are not
identical in their views of, attitudes toward, and
involvement with death and death-related issues. The
average woman encounters death at a later age than does

the average man. For that reason alone the meaning she
gives to it may be different from that which a man would
assign it. The traditional nurturing role of woman still
places her closer to the physical act of dying than is
the average man, as shown by the sex differential in the
nursing profession The biology of woman, with its inherent property of being able to bear life but also to
lose that life by chance or choice, may give her special
problems in the areas of abortion and stillbirths. The
conditioning of women, not only for nurturance but for
expression of affection, allows them to react to death
differently than do males and to express their anxieties
concerning death in the abstract more openly than do
their brothers. Woman's continuing central position in
the family may result in her being more responsible for
death education in the home than is her mate. Women's
longevity compared to men makes them more likely to be
widowed, yet their traditional socialization makes them
less likely to be able to cope effectively with the
demands of the world of the widow. In addition, the
changing role of women has implications for their continued longevity, their availability to nurture and care
for the terminally ill, as well as their choices in the
areas of abortion and euthanasia. Our task is to examine
many aspects of death with an eye toward differential
perception and behavior by the two sexes.

Chapter 2 will examine the changing statistics on longevity with particular emphasis on the increasing sex differential in death which seems to favor women. Hypotheses
concerning the factors leading to longer life for women
than for men will be suggested. Three perspectives, the
biogenetic, the psychosocial, and the environmental,
will be discussed.

Chapter 3 will look at the whole question of how women
and men differentially view the subject of death. Death
attitudes, death anxiety, and fantasies about death will
be discussed. The framework of this chapter will be a
life span perspective.

Chapter 4 will review major research findings on the
subject of violent death. Men do commit murder and
suicide more frequently than women. However, although
women have long been thought to be the passive sex,
statistics on murder, attempted murder, and suicide committed by women leave little doubt that women are not
strangers to violence. Are there differences in the
conditions under which men and women attempt to kill?
Who are their most common victims? Why do more women
than men attempt suicide while more men than women are
successful in their attempts? These and other questions
will be addressed in this chapter.

Chapter 5 is designed to explore the area of coping with loss from a life span perspective. The grief process will be examined as will sex differences in coping reactions. Special problems that women and men face in coping with the death of a child, their parents, and their mates will be discussed.

In Chapter 6 we will examine the need for death education and counseling for both sexes and all ages at this time in our culture. A general structure for carrying out death education in the home will be presented. Counseling tasks and skills for working with the bereaved will be reviewed. The similarities between death education seminars and small group therapy will be explored. Finally, a list of helpful aids for the death educator and/or counselor will be suggested.

SUMMARY

Human beings seem to have a real need to understand the concept of death. They make active efforts at understanding from a very early age. At the same time they are accumulating information concerning their gender, which often in turn colors their understanding of death-related concerns.

Myths and practices in early cultures have attributed powers over both life and death to women. In spite of, or perhaps because of, these attributions, many cultures have valued women differently from men as evidenced by the sex differential in infant killing, poor treatment of widows, and even a lower rate of inclusion in modern obituary columns.

In the last two decades the woman's movement and the death education movement have been progressing side by side and have complemented each other. Even as the woman's movement has concerned itself with equal opportunity for women to become self-actualized beings, the death education movement has reminded all humans that opportunity and development are limited by the inescapable fact of death. The purpose of this book is to examine the sex differential in longevity and death-related attitudes, behaviors, and coping skills in the hope that such an examination may add to our understanding of the worlds of both sexes even as it encourages us to become more aware of death-related issues.

REFERENCES

1. Grof, S., cited in Sagan, C., Broca's brain: Reflections on the romance of science. New York: Random House, 1979.

2. Moody, R. <u>Life after life</u>. Atlanta, Mockingbird, 1975.

3. Kohlberg, L., and Ullman, D. Stages in the develop-
    ment of psychosexual concepts and attitudes. In
    R. C. Friedman, R. M. Richart, and R. L. VandeWiele
    (Eds.), <u>Sex differences in behavior</u>, 209-222. New
    York: Wiley, 1974.

4. Harrison, J. E. <u>Myths of Greece and Rome</u>. Norwood,
    Norwood Editions, 1977, p. 70.

5. Guerber, H. A. <u>The myths of Greece and Rome</u>. Lon-
    don: Harrap, 1938.

6. <u>The new analytical Bible</u>, King James version.
    <u>Chicago: Dickson, 1950.</u>

7. Fisher, S., Wright, D., and Moelis, I. Effects of
    maternal themes upon death imagery, <u>Journal of
    Personality Assessment</u>, 1979, <u>43</u>, 6.

8. Kastenbaum, R., and Aisenburg, R. <u>The psychology
    of death</u>. New York: Springer, 1972, p. 293.

9. Hoyenga, K. B., and Hoyenga, K. T. <u>The question
    of sex differences</u>. Boston: Little, Brown, 1979.

10. Michener, J. <u>Centennial</u>. New York: Random House,
    1974.

11. Newsletter of the North Carolinians United for
    E.R.A., "What happens if this man leaves the
    picture?" Durham, N.C., 1979.

12. Kastenbaum, R. <u>Death, society and human experience</u>.
    St. Louis: Mosby, 1977.

13. Stillion, J., and Shamblin, J. Sexism in Death,
    workshop presented at Sixth Annual National Con-
    ference on Feminist Psychology, Dallas, Texas, 1979.

14. Spilka, B., Lacey, G., and Gelb, B. Sex discrimina-
    tion after death: A replication, extension and a
    difference. <u>Omega</u>, 1979-80, <u>10</u>(3), 227-233.

15. Fulton, R., Marukusen, E., Owen, G., and Scheiber,
    J. <u>Death and dying: Challenge and change</u>. Reading,
    Mass.: Addison-Wesley, 1978, p. 10.

16. Feifel, H. <u>The meaning of death</u>. New York: McGraw-
    Hill, 1959.

17. Shneidman, E. S., in Fulton, R., Markusen, E.,

Owen, G., and Scheiber, J. Death and dying: Chal-
lenge and change. Reading, Mass.: Addison-Wesley,
1978, p. 23.

18.   Braga, J., and Braga, L., in Kübler-Ross, E., Death:
      The final stage of growth. Englewood Cliffs, N.J.:
      Prentice-Hall, 1975.

SEX DIFFERENCES IN LONGEVITY

How short is human life.... The very breath which
frames my words accelerates my death.

Hannah Moore
King Hezekiah

THE CHANGING FACE OF DEATH

America is a society that prides itself on its ability
to be innovative and to adapt to change. Nevertheless,
the major changes in average life expectancy experienced
in the United States during this century have set in
motion forces that are affecting and will continue to
affect every aspect of our culture. When more than 7
percent of a nation's population are aged 65 and older,
according to demographers it becomes known as an aged
nation (1). The United States has reached that figure.
Implications for social programs, continued economic
growth, medical care, and human service specialists are
just a few of the concerns that must be addressed by
society's leaders during the remaining decades of the
twentieth century.

For thousands of years, average human longevity grew at
a snail's pace, as revealed by the information in Table
2.1. However, during this century alone, it has increased
a total of 26.4 years. Such rapid increase in life expectancy has affected more than just societal patterns.
It has changed the individual psychology of humans.
Let's examine some of the most common implications of
having a life expectancy of 70 years rather than that of
47 years, as was true at the turn of this century.

The additional quarter of a century afforded to the
average person has allowed him/her to develop different

TABLE 2.1   Life Expectancies for Humans From Prehistoric
to Contemporary Times

Time Period	Average Life Span in Years
Prehistory	18
Ancient Greece	20
Ancient Rome	22
Middle Ages, England	33
1620 (Massachusetts Bay Colony)	35
19th Century England, Wales	41
1900 USA	47.3
1915 USA	54.5*
1930 USA	59.7
1940 USA	62.9
1950 USA	68.2
1960 USA	69.7
1970 USA	70.9
1975 USA	72.5
1976 USA	72.8
1977 USA	73.2
1978 USA	73.3
1979 USA	73.7

*Source through 1915: Learner, M., The demography of death.   In
E. S. Shneidman (Ed.), Death: current perspectives.   Palo Alto,
Calif.: Mayfield, 1976, p. 140.
Source after 1915: Statistical abstract of the United States, 1981,
1982-83.   103d annual edition.   Washington, D.C.: U.S. Bureau of
the Census, 1982.

expectations about life in general.   Specifically,
greater longevity has supported the growth of the following trends in our society:

1. A delayed dependency period has evolved, during
    which biologically mature males and females remain
    within the home, usually involved in advanced learn-
    ing.   This period, known as adolescence, has engen-
    dered a whole new field of study and has resulted
    in young people between the ages of 12 and 18 devel-
    oping a specialized, transitional self-concept.
2. A prolonged period even beyond adolescence, in which
    the main task is preparation for the world of work,
    has become common.   Keniston (2) has termed this
    stage of development youth, and has pointed out that
    only relatively wealthy and long-lived cultures can
    afford to have people who are not directly producing
    either goods or services for a number of their

healthiest years--people who have not yet made a total commitment to their culture.

3. A trend toward career change in mid-life has emerged. Observers of our culture tell us that the average adult can expect to make six or seven career changes during his or her lifetime (3). Such a pattern would have been impossible in a culture in which people at age 35 could only expect a dozen more years of life.

4. A trend toward sequencing in many of life's major areas has developed. The knowledge that one may live 50 years beyond age 20 frees people to examine alternatives to their present life-style several times during adulthood. Such flexibility of thought may be partially responsible for the increased incidence of serial monogamy (being faithful to one mate for a period of time and then seeking another mate). Women, in particular, are looking to sequencing as a way of maximizing their abilities; of having it all. Many young women today, recognizing their added longevity, are planning to get an education, work for a few years before and after marriage, drop out of the labor force for a period of about five years to raise preschool children, update their vocational skills in a type of transition stage, and return to the labor force for a period of 25 to 30 years. Knowledgeable young people no longer consider raising children a full-time, life-long task for most women. They realize that after the youngest child in today's smaller families grows to adulthood, most women will still have two or more decades of active, healthy life ahead of them before their mate can join them in retirement.

5. A desire of people to find meaning in their work has become apparent. Today's adults realize they will be spending approximately 40 years in the work force, a period longer than life expectancy for most humans throughout history. Related to this trend is a liberalizing of retirement practices so that those who find personal meaning in work can work beyond age 65, and those who want to retire early and place an emphasis on effective use of leisure can be helped financially through early retirement plans to do this.

Most of these and other changing life patterns that accompany increased life expectancy have been accepted as desirable by the majority of Americans. Accompanying this century's increase in life expectancy, however, is a very interesting and highly undemocratic statistic. Table 2.2 shows that although both sexes have gained years in life expectancy, there is a sex differential in the gains which favors women. While the average woman in 1920 lived one year longer than the average man, by the year 1979, she had added almost eight more years than he to her life span.

TABLE 2.2   Expectations of Life at Birth: 1920-1979

Year	Males	Females
1920	53.6	54.6
1930	58.1	61.6
1940	60.8	65.2
1950	65.6	71.1
1955	66.7	72.8
1960	66.6	73.1
1965	66.8	73.7
1970	67.1	74.8
1971	67.4	75.0
1972	67.4	75.1
1973	67.6	75.3
1974	68.1	75.8
1975	68.7	76.5
1976	69.0	76.7
1977	69.3	77.1
1978	69.5	77.2
1979	69.9	77.6

Source: Statistical Abstract of the United States, 1982-83, 103rd
Annual Edition, U.S. Bureau of the Census, Washington, D.C., 1982.

Such a discrepancy in life expectancy between the sexes
has drawn the attention of researchers in many areas:
demography, biology, medicine, psychology, and sociology.
Research concerning this sex differential in death has
emerged from each of these fields. It can be grouped
under three major headings that we shall call the biogenetic, environmental, and psychosocial perspectives.

THE BIOGENETIC PERSPECTIVE

Let us begin at the beginning as we examine the part
genetics and biology may play in the sex difference in
mortality. The human male is responsible for the sex of
the offspring. There is every reason to believe that
adult males produce equal numbers of x-bearing (female)
sperm and y-bearing (male) sperm. In theory, at least,
there should be equal numbers of male and female infants
born. In fact, this is not true. There are approximately
106 males born for every 100 females, not only in our
culture but around the world (4).

At first glance, the predominance of male infants might
suggest healthier male prenatal development. In fact,
the reverse is true. Evidence exists that males are at
higher risk from conception on. In one study, researchers

found by examining the fetal portion of placentas available after miscarriages that the sex ratio of male to
female fetuses lost was 160.2 to 100 (5). Other researchers have indicated that there are a greater number of
male stillborn and newborn deaths compared to female
deaths in each category. The percentage of male to
female infant deaths in babies weighing over 1000 grams
in one study was 61.3 males to 38.7 females, or almost
two to one (4). Apparently, y-bearing sperm, perhaps
because they are smaller and faster, are more often successful in reaching and fertilizing the waiting ovum.
However, the ova fertilized by the y-bearing sperm are
more likely to be spontaneously aborted than those
fertilized by x-bearing sperm.

One early, well accepted study of the male-female prenatal sex ratio in mortality concluded that there are
probably 111 males conceived for every 100 females (5).
Later authors have speculated that ratio might be as
large as 120 to 100 (6). Whatever the figure, two facts
emerge from the research on the prenatal and neonatal
periods: (1) nature provided for more males than females
to be conceived, and (2) more males than females die
between conception and the end of the neonatal period
some two to four weeks after birth.

In trying to explain the excess loss of males prenatally,
two common reasons are given. The first, more an observation than an explanation, is that the human species is
similar to most of the animal kingdom in that males are
programmed for earlier death, and are therefore less
well equipped from the beginning to meet the challenges
of survival. The second attempts to look at the differential process that fetuses of both sexes must go
through. Proponents of this explanation point out that
the male fetus, between the age of 4 and 16 weeks after
conception, must undergo an additional step in order to
develop into a healthy male. Somewhere around 6 weeks
after conception, the presence of the y chromosome in
the male causes the inner part of the primitive non-
sexually differentiated organ called an ovotestis to
develop into a testis. By 8 weeks of age the ducts have
developed into male or female structures. Testicular
hormones begin to be produced in the male testis and
masculine differentiation is complete by about the six-
teenth week. The female fetus does not have to undergo
a separate feminizing process (7). In the absence of
fetal male hormone, the ovotestis develops into ovaries,
and the baby develops a normal female anatomy. Spontaneous
abortions often occur in the presence of a genetic or
developmental abnormality. Physicians tell us that
abortions are nature's way of correcting mistakes. Since
male in utero development is more complicated than female
development, perhaps the greater number of male spontaneous abortions reflects the more hazardous sexual
developmental pattern.

TABLE 2.3   Number of Deaths Per 100,000 Males and
Females - 1981

Age (years)	Male	Female
Under 1	1,345	1,029
1 - 4	68	52
5 - 14	39	22
15 - 24	159	55
25 - 34	198	77
35 - 44	302	156
45 - 54	761	408
55 - 64	1,784	942
65 - 74	4,013	2,115
75 - 84	8,526	5,186
85	18,238	14,089

Source: Statistical Abstract of the United States, 1982-83, 103rd
Edition, U.S. Bureau of the Census, Washington, D.C., 1982, p. 73.

Continuing beyond infancy, if we examine recent figures
of death rates by sex, we find that the male is at
higher risk of death in every age group across the life
span.   Table 2.3 makes the point effectively.

In considering causes of the sex differential in death,
we must remember that the earlier the loss occurs, the
less the likelihood that it could be influenced by
socialization, although environmental factors, even in
utero, cannot be completely eliminated as adding to the
mortality rate.   If biology does play a major role in
the sex differential in mortality after birth, what
mechanism may be involved?

People sharing the biogenetic perspective hypothesize
that one possible cause of the sex differential in
mortality across the life span is the fact that the y
chromosome carries less information than does the x.
Some supporters of this view describe the y chromosome
as an incomplete x chromosome.   They point to the existence of over 50 conditions that have been found almost
exclusively in males and have been caused by x-linked
recessive genes (8).   These conditions occur because the
y chromosome lacks the necessary dominant genetic material
to balance and cancel the faulty, recessive information
being carried on the larger x chromosome.   Such conditions
include hemophilia, one type of diabetes, one form of
muscular dystrophy, and some types of metabolic disorders
(9).

Other supporters of the biogenetic perspective point out
that the x chromosome carries numbers of genes which help
produce a substance known as immunoglobulin M. This
substance aids in protection against many types of diseases. It would follow, therefore, that males would be
more susceptible to many diseases than would females.
Furthermore, estrogens and progesterone, the two major
female hormones, seem to stimulate a cleansing action in
the body while testosterone does not (8).

Still other supporters of the biogenetic perspective
point to increased metabolic rate for males as a factor
feeding into earlier death. Conrad wrote,

> It is assumed that the male is inherently more
> active, consumes more energy, is physically
> stronger, but dies at an earlier age than the
> female who is less active, consumes less food,
> but conserves more energy and consequently
> lives longer. (10, p. 195)

Other authors point to life habits based on biological
differences in metabolism as adding to the sex differential, in death. For example, if male metabolic rate
demands a higher intake of food, water, and even sugar
(for quick energy), and if those substances--either
naturally or through increased levels of environmental
pollutants--are carcinogenic, the male would be at
higher risk in developing cancer than would the female.
Indeed, in all types of cancer, except for breast and
uterine cancer, the male does have a higher rate (8).

Perhaps the best-known study supporting the biogenetic
perspective was done by Madigan (11), who compared
Brothers and Sisters of religious orders whose life-styles
were similar. He believed that choosing this particular
group for research resulted in a study in which "socio-
cultural stresses have been greatly standardized between
the sexes" (p. 208). The males in this population were
more protected than the general population of males,
while the career-minded females in this population at
least at this time were under more stress than the
average middle-class homemaker. Therefore he reasoned
that if the sex differential in death in this population
were the same as that in the general population, he
would have found support for a biological component in
death differential.

Madigan concluded that:

> (1) Biological factors are MORE important
> than sociocultural pressures and strains in
> relation to the differential sex death rates;
> and (2) that the greater sociocultural stresses
> associated with the male role in our society play

only a small and unimportant part in producing
the differentials between male and female death
rates (11, p. 209).

THE ENVIRONMENTAL PERSPECTIVE

Criticism of Madigan's work and opposition to the biogenetic perspective it seemed to support were not long
in coming. Critics pointed out, for example, that
Madigan's male subjects smoked significantly more than
did his female subjects and that other variables such as
sex role socialization, amount of exercise, amount of
alcohol consumed, etc., had not been systematically
studied (8, 12). Environmental factors, critics maintained, play a significant if not the most significant
role in explaining the sex differential in death.
Supporters of the environmental position maintain that
there are at least seven major external factors that
feed into the sex differential in death. These include
health technology, nature of work and working conditions,
smoking, diet, body weight in relation to height, exercise,
and stress (12). Let us examine each of these factors
briefly.

The most obvious environmental source of improved life
expectancy for all people is that of advancement in
health technology and medical practices. Remember that
life expectancy refers to the number of years an average
individual can expect to live rather than to ultimate
longevity, i.e., the oldest age anyone has reached.
Gains in life expectancy are relatively easy to realize,
while no real gains in ultimate longevity have been
recorded.

Much of the improvement in overall life expectancy has
resulted from reductions in infant mortality coupled with
reduced maternal postpartum deaths and fewer deaths from
childhood diseases (12). The reduction in infant mortality is in turn related to better nutrition, prenatal
care, and improved methods of childbirth. However,
improved infant mortality rates should benefit male and
female infants equally and therefore shed little light
on the sex differential in death.

The decline in maternal deaths is related to a decrease
in complications such as puerperal (childbirth) fever
and hemorrhage as well as to more informed family planning
and wider use of more effective contraceptive techniques.
Increased knowledge about the importance of antiseptic
conditions and balanced rest and exercise after delivery
coupled with the discovery of penicillin have also helped
to decrease the complications of childbirth. Obviously,
if more mothers survive childbirth they will live to a
greater age, thus feeding into the favorable female sex

differential in death. This factor may then be a real
one from an environmental perspective in increasing
female life expectancy over that of males.

Deaths from childhood diseases have also decreased,
largely as a result of a widely implemented program of
inoculation against the major disease killers. In the
past century researchers have discovered how to prevent
diphtheria, pertussis, typhoid fever, smallpox, and polio
as well as the more accepted but often fatal or maiming
illnesses of measles and mumps. Once again however,
such discoveries should increase the life expectancies
of males and females equally. Although they may explain
greater overall human longevity, they are not helpful in
explaining the increased sex differential in death.

The second major environmental factor is related to the
changing nature of work in this century. The old adage,
"A man's work lasts from sun to sun, but a woman's work
is never done," is not quite as true today as it was at
the turn of the century. Technical innovations in labor-
saving devices, while not dramatically reducing the total
number of hours that full-time homemakers devote to house-
work, have lightened the nature of that work. The image
of the frontier woman who literally worked herself to
death at an early age, trapped in a life of physical
drudgery, has become less common in our culture. Therefore, women may be realizing additional years as a result
of the changing nature of their work even if the hours
they spend working may not have been significantly reduced.

A factor related to the nature of work is that of place
of work. Women, in comparison to men, have traditionally
worked in cleaner, safer, more comfortable environments.
Consider the traditional "big three" career options for
women: teaching, secretarial work, and nursing. All
three share in common with homemaking the fact that they
are located indoors, away from hazardous physical conditions (with the possible exception of some types of
nursing), and are relatively free from inherently dangerous job requirements. Contrast the environment of
"women's work" to that of many jobs that are viewed as
traditionally male: coal mining, test piloting, being a
fireman, policeman, race car driver, high-rise construction
worker, for example. War, perhaps the most extreme
example of danger in the workplace, has claimed 426,000
male lives in this century alone. Such a contrast indicates that work environment may be a real factor in the
increasing sex differential in death. However, if
vocational options continue to increase for women as
they have begun to do in the past decade, this source of
input into the sex differential may result in a decrease
in women's longevity.

The next environmental factor to be examined is that of
cigarette smoking. In a detailed mathematical analysis,
Retherford concluded that cigarette smoking alone seems
to account for between 47 and 75 percent of the total
sex differential in death, depending upon the age of the
people studied (12). Certainly, the Surgeon General of
the United States has attempted to warn the public both
by disseminating reports and by the warning mandated on
all cigarette packages that he "has determined that
cigarette smoking is dangerous to your health." While
we have included cigarette smoking as an environmental
factor, we will examine it once again under psychosocial
causes of the sex differential. The reason why intelligent human beings choose to engage knowingly in a life-
threatening behavior appears to be rooted as much in
the psyche as in the environment.

The factors of diet, body weight in relation to height,
and exercise will be considered as a triad that may be
slightly responsible for the increase in the sex differential in death. In the early part of this century, the
idealized image of women changed from the hourglass
figure that Rubens and other artists had idealized to
the flat-chested "flapper" image of the 1920s. Females
were known to bind their breasts in order to attain the
boy-like or immature girl-like figure then in vogue,
and well-endowed women found themselves out of style.
While recent fashion has not seemed so extreme as the
flapper image, slimness is still the feminine ideal.
"No one can be too rich or too slim," an unknown woman
quipped recently. Women have a 60-year history of
watching their weight and of combining diet and exercise
so as to maintain their "girlish figures." They have
been aided in this behavior by being in charge of the
grocery buying, menu planning, and cooking and are
generally more knowledgeable than are men about the components of balanced meals. Women also tend to eat
lighter meals with more vegetables and fruits than do
men. In recent years, however, our society has experienced
a new emphasis on body image and exercise by males as
well as by females, and an increased interest in cooking
by males. To the extent that diet, body weight in relation to height, and exercise are real factors in longevity, we may see men making gains in the near future,
resulting in closing the gap between male and female
life expectancies.

The factor of stress, suggested by Retherford (12) as
important to the sex differential, has traditionally
been interpreted as causing early male deaths because
males are supposed to live in a more stressful environment. We will examine the way in which stress may affect
longevity in detail in the next section. However, it is
important to note here that research in the area of
environmental stress as it affects health is incomplete

and contradictory. For example, deaths from coronary
heart disease actually decreased in occupied countries
during World War II. Common wisdom might hypothesize
that environmental stress would be higher in occupied
than in nonoccupied countries. Also, it is far from
clear that the male role, especially at this time in
history, is more inherently stressful than that of the
female. To the extent that environmental stress alone
decreases longevity, we might expect to see females'
life expectancies growing shorter as females find themselves fulfilling the same types of roles as men while
still trying to retain their traditional roles as well.

An environmental factor not suggested by Retherford that
we must consider is that of socioeconomic status (13).
The old song lyric, "the rich get richer and the poor
get poorer," seems to apply to mortality as well as
finances. Wealthier people live longer. They can afford
better health care and may have a more leisurely, less
stressful life-style. They can also afford to eat well.
In addition, wealthier people frequently have more education and are therefore more knowledgeable about the needs
of their bodies. Knowledge, coupled with the financial
capacity to implement it, is a winning combination in
the longevity race. Once again, however, as was the
case with decreased infant and child mortality, this
factor does not help us greatly in understanding the sex
differential in longevity. While one might make an
argument for the supposition that traditionally wealthy
females have an even more leisurely, less stressful
existence than do comparable males, evidence to support
this position is not available.

The final environmental factor we should consider is
that of marital status. It has been shown that married
people of both sexes live longer (13). There is no
doubt that married people tend to live more structured
and more regular lives than do the single, widowed, or
divorced. Marriage also may provide close, meaningful
social ties that some believe are inversely related to
mortality statistics. Gove (1979), in making a case for
the positive relationship between marriage and longevity,
points out that

> The shift from being single to being married
> appears from the mortality rates, to have a
> more favorable effect on men than on women,
> while the shift from the married to an unmar-
> ried state appears to have a more unfavorable
> effect on men than on women. For men, being un-
> married is uniformly associated with mortality
> rates that are higher than those of the married
> with the widowed and divorced having especially
> high rates. (14, p. 53)

The environmental factor of marital status may affect
the sex differential but not in the clear-cut ways we
have seen in the other environmental factors. Married
men may live longer than single men. Married women may
have a lesser (but still positive) addition to their
life span than do married men. When the overall average
is taken of married, widowed, divorced, and single men,
however, it still results in shorter longevity than the
overall average for the same categories of women. In
summary, men seem to find marriage more beneficial to
their physical health than do women and singlehood more
disadvantageous, but the overall impact of marital status
cannot help us much in understanding the sex differential
in death.

Overall, the environmental position is interesting, and
undeniably some of the factors discussed above do enter
into the sex differential in death. Taken alone, however,
the environmentalist position does not explain such
puzzles as why men have 30 percent more automobile
accidents per mile driven than do females, or why they
experience 130 percent more fatal accidents per mile
driven (15). Driving is dangerous, but it should be
equally dangerous to both sexes if one controls for the
amount of driving done. Nor does the environmentalist
position explain why men choose jobs in unsafe circumstances more frequently than do women and why they then
allow the job setting to remain hazardous, rather than
working to improve the safety of the workplace. In
order to develop a real understanding of the factors
behind the accident statistics as well as the increased
suicide and disease rates for males, it is necessary to
examine the psychosocial perspective.

THE PSYCHOSOCIAL PERSPECTIVE

What we are calling the psychosocial perspective views
human beings as both active and reactive within their
life space. It maintains that individuals develop
relatively stable personalities as they attempt to organize their ever-increasing knowledge of the social world
around them into a meaningful psychological whole. One
of the very first categories about self that children
learn is gender. We will look at the process and impact
of this learning in more detail in Chapter 3. Suffice
it to say here that men and women learn different norms
of behavior and that these norms, once internalized,
affect values, attitudes, and options for each sex.
Let's take a look at what some male authors have to say
about the key messages learned by males in our culture.

Goldberg, in The Hazards of Being Male, pointed out that
boys learn early that to be a real man, you must be the
strong, silent, independent type (16). Jourard summed

up the socially prescribed male role as one which requires
males to be noncommunicative, competitive, and nongiving
as well as inexpressive. Males are taught to evaluate
life success in terms of external achievements rather
than personal and interpersonal fulfillment (17). David
and Brannon (18) discussed the central messages of the
stereotyped male sex role by using the following short-
hand. Males, they said, are taught four primary impera-
tives:

1. "No sissy stuff": this involves the need to be
    different from women in every dimension possible.
2. "Be a big wheel": this involves the need to be
    superior to others, necessitating a competitive
    rather than a cooperative life-style.
3. "Be a sturdy oak": this involves the need to be
    independent and self-reliant, traits that we will
    examine in more detail later as possible contributors
    to early death for males.
4. "Give 'em hell": this involves the need to be more
    powerful than others, through violence if necessary,
    and creates the foundation for hostility, aggression,
    and ruthlessness as a way of life. All of these
    messages have direct implications both for longevity
    and for life satisfaction.

In order to explore more fully the differential impact
of norms and sex roles on men and women, let us look
individually at the seven major causes of higher mortality
in men cited by Waldron in her classic article (8).
Table 2.4 lists all causes of death in which males had
at least twice as high a mortality rate as did females
and which were responsible for at least 1 percent of all
deaths in the United States in 1967. Waldron calculates
that these causes were responsible for three-quarters of
the sex differential in death in that year.

The leading cause of higher mortality in men than in
women is malignant neoplasm of the respiratory system
followed closely by other bronchopulmonic diseases
(mainly emphysema). Both of these categories are directly
affected by two major variables: cigarette smoking and
industrial pollution. The question we must examine from
the psychosocial point of view is why more males than
females smoke and why more males do not insist on higher
safety and health standards in their occupational environments. Two of the most commonly heard reasons for
beginning to smoke are that it is "macho" and that it
serves to relieve tension in what has been until recently
a socially approved manner. Think for a moment about the
last few advertisements you have seen for cigarettes.
Smoking males are still being portrayed as rugged out-
doorsmen or as sophisticated romantic men, knowledgeable
in the ways of pleasing a woman. In either case, young
males have traditionally been attracted to smoking because

TABLE 2.4   Major Causes of Higher Mortality in Men

Ratio of Male to Female Death Rates	Cause of Death	Male Death Rate	Female Death Rate[a]
		(Deaths 100,000 population)	
5.9	Malignant neo-plasm of respir-atory system, not specified as secondary	50.1	8.5
4.9	Other broncho-pulmonic disease (71% emphysema)	24.4	5.0
2.8	Motor vehicle accidents	39.4	14.2
2.7	Suicide	15.7	5.8
2.4	Other accidents	41.1	17.4
2.0	Cirrhosis of liver	18.5	9.1
2.0	Arteriosclerotic heart disease, including coronary disease	357.0	175.6
1.6	All causes	1981.7	657.0

This table lists all causes of death which had a sex mortality ratio of 2.0 or more and were responsible for at least 1% of all deaths in the U.S. in 1967. These causes of death are responsible for three quarters of the sex differential in mortality (calculated from data in (98)).

[a]Female death rates have been age-adjusted using the age specific death rates for females and the age distribution for males to cal-culate the death rate which would be expected for a population of females that had the same age distribution as the male population. Thus the male and female death rates are directly comparable and are not affected by the higher proportion of females at older ages.

Source: Waldron, I. Why do women live longer than men, Social Science and Medicine, 1976, 10, 349-362.

it presented the secure, healthy, robust, and knowledge-able image that they wished to attain. But what has this to do with men continuing to work in industries that they know have been hazardous to their health without attempt-ing to change them? Could it be that a real "man's man" is not expected to complain; that he is expected to prove his masculinity on a day-to-day basis by surviving and producing in less than optimum conditions? And could it be that men learn this lesson so early and so

thoroughly that in some perverse way they take pride in
risking their health in a so-called masculine environment?

The next three categories in Table 2.4 seem irrevocably
tied to the traditional male sex role as discussed. The
category of motor vehicle accidents and other accidents,
for example, may reflect the qualities of dominance and
competition which are thought to be masculine qualities.
Even when we acknowledge that males drive more and drive
during the congested times of the day more than do females,
we cannot explain away the troubling accident statistics.
How much of the increased death rate in accidents for
males might be caused by that competitive urge to "get
ahead of that guy in front of me," or by the desire to
"cut just a few minutes off my last time to work"; not
to mention the time-honored tradition of proving one's
masculinity by "playing chicken"?

The higher incidence of male suicide might well be related to the first category which Brannon mentions: "No
sissy stuff." Females attempt suicide twice as frequently
as do males, but males are significantly more successful
than are females, as is seen in Table 2.4. For one
thing, males use more violent means such as guns, knives,
and hanging. However, since males are more successful
suicides in every method used than are females, method
alone cannot explain the difference (9). Could it be
that males' socialization messages are still functioning
in times of severe stress, blotting out even the strong
urge toward survival? The male, facing depression,
failure, or loss may be attending to sex role messages
even as he contemplates suicide. Such messages as,
"Take your medicine like a man," "Be a man about this,"
or even, "Big boys don't cry," may partially account for
the higher male success rate in suicide. Furthermore,
it seems as though the achievement motive might be
operating here. A large volume of research accumulated
by McClelland and his associates over the past two decades
indicates that the achievement motive in males is strong
and linear (19-21). That is, men know that they are
expected to strive to produce and do well from an early
age. Success is the goal; failure undermines masculinity.
Perhaps stressed males are applying the achievement
motive when contemplating suicide. Women can and do use
suicide as a call for help. Men more frequently plan and
carry out suicide in such a way that it cannot fail. One
emergency room nurse sharing her experience with this
phenomenon said, "Most men when they regain consciousness
after a suicide attempt will say, 'You mean I failed in
this, too? I can't do anything right'." She commented
that the humiliation the men felt over failing in their
suicide attempts seemed to bother them as much as or more
than whatever originally precipitated the attempts. The
category of other accidents may reflect once again the
messages of "No sissy stuff" and "Be a big wheel." Just

as Tom Sawyer proved his masculinity by walking on top
of fences and exploring farther than did the other boys,
today's males may be forced into similar dangerous
situations at every age (22).

The next category of higher male than female death as
revealed in Table 2.4 is cirrhosis of the liver. While
not always caused by alcohol consumption, cirrhosis is
highly related to it. Alcohol and other drugs may serve
as one of the few escapes for the "sturdy oak"-type male.
If a male learns early that he must be independent and
self-reliant at all times, he may turn to alcohol to
help him "take the edge off" his socialization so that
he can allow himself to communicate; or, he may lose
himself in alcohol so as to flee his loneliness and
psychological isolation.

The final category in Table 2.4 is that of arteriosclerotic heart disease. Smoking and faulty diet resulting
in elevated cholesterol and triglycerides seem to play
a role in this category as does the general area of
stress. How does the male sex role relate to diet?
Goldberg (23), in a recent presentation, suggested that
there is "male food" and there is "female food". He
maintained that the typical husky truck driver who
entered the truck stop and ordered a small salad and
iced tea would be ridiculed even though it would probably
be a healthier meal for him than a huge steak and beer
or a cheeseburger with greasy fries. The popularity of
the tongue-in-cheek best seller Real Men Don't Eat Quiche
indicates widespread recognition that male eating habits
tend to conform to men's self-concept.

The effect of stress on arteriosclerotic heart disease
can best be understood within the context of the research
done on Type A and Type B personalities. We have seen
that research on the relationship of stress to death is
equivocal. Perhaps this is because stress in itself is
neither good nor bad. Selye has made a case for the
fact that some stress is energizing, propelling us to
perform at maximum capacity. Such stress he terms
"eustress" (24). Much of the effect of stress depends
on how we as individuals react to the forces around us.
Our personalities, largely organized around our understanding of sex and its appropriate role behavior, may
interact with stressors in the environment to increase
coronary heart disease. Let's examine supporting evidence
for this hypothesis.

Two cardiologists at Mt. Zion Hospital in San Francisco
have been carrying out a longitudinal study on 3500
middle-aged corporate men who had no known history of
coronary problems at the inception of the study (25, 26).
About half of the group was characterized as having

TABLE 2.5   Age Adjusted Death Rate for Males Compared to
Females by Disease - 1979

Cause of Death	%
Diseases of the heart	2.0
Malignant neoplasms	1.5
Cerebrovascular diseases	1.8
Accidents and adverse effects	3.0
Motor vehicle accidents	3.0
All other accidents	3.0
Pulmonary diseases	3.1
Pneumonia and influenza	1.9
Chronic liver diseases and cirrhosis	2.2
Atherosclerosis	1.3
Suicide	3.1
Homicide	3.9
Nephritis	1.6
Septicemia	1.4

Source: Monthly Vital Statistics, 3(6), Supplement. September 30,
1982. Washington, D.C.: U.S. Department of Health and Human
Services, 1982.

Type A personalities.   According to Rosenman and
Friedman, the Type A behavior pattern results from

> a combination of certain personality traits
> such as excessive competitive "drive," per-
> sistent desire for recognition, advancement
> and achievement, and persistent inclination
> for multiple vocational and avocational involve-
> ments on the one hand, and of chronic immersion
> in "deadlines" on the other hand.... The key
> area of harassment in such an individual
> usually is a seeming paucity of time itself.
> (25, p. 1173)

Certainly, this description echoes the message involved
in Brannon's "Be a big wheel" category.

After eight years of the study, 257 of the executives
had developed heart disease.   Of that number, 70 percent
had been classified Type A at an earlier time.   Type A
behavior has come to be known as coronary prone behavior.
Although women can be and are classified as Type A,
Rosenman and Friedman found that Type A men outnumber
Type A women even among populations where women are
employed in approximately equal types of positions.
Perhaps the male who becomes convinced at an early age
that his entire worth and identity are tied up with his

ability to produce will be more likely to become Type A
in his behavior pattern. Large studies of men who display
Type A behavior have shown that these men are twice as
likely as other men not evidencing this behavior to
develop or die of coronary heart disease. Indeed Rosenman
and his colleagues have maintained that possessing Type
A characteristics may be a more important indication of who
will develop heart disease than is any other factor,
including diet, exercise, and even smoking.

Table 2.5 represents age-adjusted death rates for males
compared to females for all causes of death for which
sex differentials were reported in the advance report
of final mortality statistics in 1979. It can be seen
that although the ratios have changed in 12 years, all
of Waldron's original categories still show increased
death rates for males over females.

WHERE DOES TRUTH LIE?

We have examined three conflicting perspectives regarding
the sex differential in mortality. All the data are not
yet in. Indeed, there are some early indications that
female longevity may be decreasing as more females smoke
cigarettes and engage in other changes in traditional
sex role behaviors (27, 8). However, at present it
appears that the best model for understanding the sex
differential in death is a complex one incorporating all
three of the perspectives discussed. The human female,
like the female of many species, may have a genetic predisposition toward a slightly longer life span. Given
the hazards of childbirth over the centuries, it would
seem properly cautious of nature to build in this slight
advantage so as to assure survival of the species. Human
beings differ from other animals, though, in their
extreme ability to help create their own living environments. The environments that they create almost always
reflect their understanding of what human males' and
females' places should be in the world. Humans have
traditionally created different worlds for males than for
females, and the female world has been less environmentally
dangerous and less demanding of physical confrontations,
resulting in fewer deaths from accidents and murder.
The female world has also been one in which she was psychologically free to express her problems and to reach out
for help with a minimum of disapproval from society, in
comparison to the male. This "safety valve" of self-
expression has probably been a factor in the increasing
longevity of women. The facts that women traditionally
have not been socialized to orient themselves toward
external success and that they can allow themselves to
fail in the eyes of the world probably feed into the
types of methods chosen for suicide attempts as well as
the lower incidence of Type A behavior in women. We are

not suggesting that longevity by itself is a goal to be pursued. As many feminists have reminded us in recent years, quality of life is at least as important as quantity. However, as we shall see in more detail in the next chapter, traditional sex role socialization of women is probably as much a factor in women's longevity and their attitudes toward death as is either biology or environment.

SUMMARY

In this chapter we have examined the changing life span of the human species in this century and some of its causes. We have also noted the existence of an inequitable sex differential in death favoring males. We have examined the major causes of death which feed into the sex differential and have suggested possible explanations of them from three perspectives: the biogenetic, the environmental, and the psychosocial. Finally, the suggestion has been made that understanding of the sex differential in death can occur only by understanding that all three of the perspectives discussed interact to create different and separate life experiences for men and for women, and that the man's life experience has traditionally been more dangerous to his physical health across the life span.

REFERENCES

1. Hendricks, J., & Hendricks, C. D. Aging in mass society: Myths and realities. Cambridge, Mass.: Winthrop, 1977.

2. Keniston, K. The uncommitted: Alienated youth in American society. New York: Harcourt, Brace & World, 1965.

3. Toffler, A. Future shock. New York: Random House, 1970.

4. Tricomi, U., Serr, D., & Solish, G. The ratio of male to female embryos as determined by the sex chromatin. American Journal of Obstetrics & Gynecology, 1960, 79, 504-509.

5. Kohl, S. G. Perinatal mortality in New York City: Responsible factors study of 1955 deaths by sub-committee on neonatal mortality, committee on public health relations, New York Academy of Medicine. Cabridge, Mass.: published for the Commonwealth Fund by Harvard University Press, 1955.

6. Ounsted, M. Gender and intrauterine growth with a

note on the use of the sex proband as a research
tool. In C. Ounsted & D. C. Taylor (Eds.), Gender
differences: Their ontogeny and significance.
London: Churchill Livingston, 1972.

7. McCary, J. L. Human sexuality: Physiological,
psychological and sociological factors (2nd ed.).
New York: Von Nostrand, 1973.

8. Waldron, I. Why do women live longer than men?
Social Science and Medicine, 1976, 10, 349-362.

9. Hoyenga, K. B., & Hoyenga, K. T. The question of
sex differences: Psychological, cultural and biological issues. Boston: Little, Brown, 1979.

10. Conrad, F. A. Sex roles as factors in longevity.
Sociology and Social Research, 1962, 46, 195-202.

11. Madigan, F. C. Are sex mortality differentials
biologically caused? Millbank Memorial Fund
Quarterly, 1957, 35, 202-213.

12. Retherford, R. The changing sex differential in
mortality. Westport, Conn.: Greenwood Press, 1975.

13. Kitagawa, E. M. On mortality. Demography, 1977,
14, 381-389.

14. Gove, W. Sex marital status and mortality. American
Journal of Sociology, 1979, 1, 45-67.

15. National Safety Council--Accident Facts, 1972.
Chicago: National Safety Council, 1972.

16. Goldberg, H. The hazards of being male: Surviving
the myth of masculine privilege. New York: Signet,
New American Library, 1977.

17. Jourard, S. The transparent self (rev. ed.).
Princeton, N.J.: Van Nostrand, 1971.

18. David, D. S., & Brannon, R. The forty-nine percent
majority: The male sex role. Reading, Mass.:
Addison-Wesley, 1976.

19. McClelland, D. C., Atkinson, J. W., Clark, R. A.,
& Lowell, F. L. The achievement motive. New York:
Appleton-Century Crofts, 1953.

20. McClelland, D. C. The achieving society. Princeton,
N.J.: Van Nostrand, 1961.

21. McClelland, D. C. Power: The inner experience.
New York: Halsted, 1975.

22. Twain, Mark. Tom Sawyer. New York: Heritage, 1936.

23. Goldberg, H. The hazards of being male. Presentation
to Asheville workshop entitled The New Male. Asheville, N.C.: 1979.

24. Selye, H. Stress without distress. Philadelphia:
Lippincott, 1974.

25. Rosenman, R. H., & Friedman, M. Association of
specific behavior pattern in women with blood and
cardiovascular findings. Circulation, 1961, 24,
1173.

26. Rosenman, R. H. The role of behavior patterns and
neurogenic factors in the pathogenesis of coronary
heart disease. In R. S. Eliot (Ed.), Stress and the
heart. Mount Kisco, N.Y.: Future, 1974.

27. Engel, H. J., Page, H. L., & Campbell, W. B. Coronary artery disease in young women. Journal of
American Medical Association, 1974, 230, 1531-1534.

3

SEX ROLES AND DEATH ATTITUDES ACROSS THE LIFE SPAN

Since men are not able to fight against death, misery and ignorance, they have taken it into their heads in order to be happy, not to think of them at all.

Pascal
Pensees

UNDERSTANDING ATTITUDE FORMATION

Attitudes are important factors in determining our behaviors throughout out lifetimes. Every attitude has three components: cognitive, affective, and behavioral. Think of the word "spinach." When you read the word "spinach," you understand it to mean a leafy green vegetable. You probably also know other things about it; for example, that it is nutritionally good for you, that it can be purchased fresh, canned, or frozen, and that it can be eaten raw or cooked in a variety of ways. Further, images of a spinach-fortified Popeye may have occurred as you read the word "spinach." All of these understandings are cognitive or fact-based aspects of your attitude toward spinach. You probably also had an affective reaction to the word. No one I know is luke-warm about spinach. They either like it very much or dislike it with equal intensity. This "ugh" or "ummm" reaction to the word spinach is the affective or feeling component referred to above. Finally, assuming that spinach is part of your next meal's menu, the behavioral part of your attitude toward spinach will be observable. Assuming that you are at least moderately hungry, you will either eat the spinach or leave it. If hungry enough, you might eat it even if you dislike it, allowing outside observers to note the affective component of your attitude toward the vegetable as you either eat it with gusto or grimace as you force it down.

Any concept we look at will contain the three elements
we have examined: cognitive, affective, and behavioral.
For the purposes of this chapter we need to examine three
words in the light of the elements of attitudes. They
are the words "male," "female," and "death." We will
look first at how we as children begin to understand the
words male and female. Based on traditional understandings of what it means to be male or female, we will make
some predictions concerning differential attitudes toward
death by the sexes. We will then examine the development
of the concept of death and the relevant literature on
death attitudes to see if predictions based on our understanding of male-female socialization are supported by
research.

BECOMING FEMALE AND MALE: THE DEVELOPMENT OF GENDER IDENTITY

Gender identity refers to the individual's experience
of her/himself as female or male and its resulting
implications for behavior and cognitive organization
of the world. Gender role, sometimes also called sex
role, refers to the outward expression of the individual's
experience of being male or female (1). There is good
evidence that gender identity is one of the earliest
understandings that a child attains. Kohlberg and Ullman
(2), following the Piagetian tradition, believe that
there are specific levels of cognition or thought processes in the development of gender identity. These
processes occur partly as a result of maturation (i.e.,
the unfolding of higher levels of understanding and
ability) and partly because of environmental influences.
In this way, children pass through levels in which they
are able to understand successively more about what it
means to be a female or a male. This understanding is
moderated by their experience in a society which either
reinforces or punishes their sex-appropriate or sex-
inappropriate behaviors.

Kohlberg states that there are five stages in the
acquisition of gender identity. The first stage of
development stresses consistency. It lasts from birth
to approximately 3 years of age and is marked by the
child's attempts to be systematic in incorporating new
information that agrees with that which he already
understands. Children at this age have little or no
understanding about what it means to be a boy or a girl,
although by age 2 they usually can correctly identify
their sex. Just as small children can count from 1 to
10 without understanding the meaning behind the numbers,
so a 2-year-old can identify his/her sex correctly but
without any real depth of understanding about what it
means. Two- and 3-year-olds will often play with toys
of the opposite sex and still enjoy engaging in cross-

sex behaviors. This kind of play can often cause parents,
especially those traditionally oriented, a great deal of
worry.

For example, Mrs. Lowe, the mother of Adam, age 2 1/2,
went to see a developmental psychologist last December.
She felt she was caught in a real bind at home. Her son
wanted a baby buggy and a doll baby for Christmas. Her
husband, an Army officer, forbade it on the grounds that
"real boys don't play with dolls." Mrs. Lowe had taken
Adam to see Santa Claus three times. On each occasion
she had rehearsed him in what he should ask for: Lego
building blocks, a Tonka truck, and a riding toy. Each
time Adam had dutifully recited the list to Santa and
then added, "But what I really, really want is a doll
baby and buggy." The Santas never promised the doll
baby and buggy. The widespread mistrust of boys playing
with girls' toys even at this age caused each Santa to
look at the mother and mutter something indefinite like,
"We'll have to see about that." Nevertheless, Mrs. Lowe
felt that Adam would be disappointed and might lose
faith in Santa Claus if he didn't get the buggy and doll
he wanted.

The psychologist pointed out that Adam was just beginning
to understand what it meant to be a boy; that he had not
yet clearly differentiated between boy toys and girl
toys, and that doll babies and buggies, after the newness
wears off, are not inherently interesting toys. She
advised Mrs. Lowe to buy the cheapest model of each and
add these to the "real boy" Christmas she had already
planned. On Christmas day, Adam ran down the stairs,
spied the doll baby and buggy, and shouted, "Santa did
remember!" He put the baby in the buggy, wheeled it
around the room once or twice, and began to explore his
other gifts. Mrs. Lowe later reported that within two
weeks a wheel had come loose on the buggy and that Adam
seemed to have no interest in it anymore.

If Adam had been a year older, he most likely would not
have asked for the doll and buggy. Kohlberg points out
that from around age 3 to age 4, children begin to value
the emerging self and thus seek out appropriate sex-typed
toys and activities because they enhance their positive
feelings of self as good. Research has shown that by
age 4, children in our culture already know what toys
are stereotypically appropriate for their sex (3).
Children at this age, however, still have not attained
what Piaget called the concept of object constancy, i.e.,
the knowledge that objects cannot magically change shape
or size on their own. Therefore, many children at this
age still believe that they can grow up to be members of
the opposite sex or that they can change their sex by
changing their appearance, e.g., by putting on a wig or
a dress.

In the third stage, which lasts from around age 4 to age 6, gender constancy (a form of object constancy) is attained and children can no longer be fooled by wigs or clothes. It is telling that Kohlberg's research shows that both boys and girls begin to associate prestige, competence, and "goodness" with the male gender role while they associate "niceness" and attractiveness with the female gender role (2). This stage may be the one in which the dictum "men must do while women must only be" becomes established.

The fourth stage lasts from approximately 6 to 7 years of age and is one of great conformity. Engaging in cross-sex behavior, e.g., boys playing with paper dolls or girls pretending to be construction workers, is seen as almost immoral. Societal expectations for males and females are taken very seriously at this stage as children attempt to work out the "good girl-good boy" dictates of this stage and play by the rules as they understand them.

The last stage, according to Kohlberg, may also start as early as 5 or 6 but continues well into the future. Between the ages of 5 and 8, children begin to model on adults who are perceived as having power, competency, and prestige and who are like themselves in some important way. Gender may be the most obvious and often used criterion for judging sameness. After about age 7 both sexes tend to view sex typing as occurring as part of the natural order of the universe. Since both boys and girls are authority-oriented at this time, they believe sex typing is the way things should be simply because it's the way things are. Since Kohlberg does not indicate further growth in gender identity, it is assumed that most adults are in this fifth stage of development, regarding traditional sex role socialization as the proper and God-given order of the universe.

Rebecca, Hefner, and Oleshansky, in an article entitled "A Model of Sex-Role Transcendence," basically support Kohlberg's work but suggest that in a free society, people may be able to move beyond differentiated sex roles to adopt life-styles that incorporate the best of the traditional male role with the best of the traditional female role to promote the fullest potential of each human being (4). They suggest a sixth stage, which can only be reached by those who have developed the highest levels of cognitive development. This stage, called sex role transcendence, cannot be reached before age 11 or 12 and then only by those people who find encouragement in their environment to move beyond stereotypic notions of gender identity and gender role. It is the stage at which people become free to experience and express the qualities stereotypically associated with both sexes; that is, to be both independent and nurturant, yielding and assertive as the situation demands. The ability to reflect a wide range of behaviors appropriate to specific situations in a flexible manner and without regard to whether the behavior in question is acceptable or appropriate to our gender is what many writers have called androgyny.

IMPLICATIONS OF GENDER IDENTITY AND ROLE FOR DEATH ATTITUDES

We have seen that children develop their gender identities and role behaviors in a sequential way that is related to their level of cognitive development. Let's now explore what possible implications traditional gender roles may have for death attitudes.

If Kohlberg is correct in his view that children believe that sex typing is the correct and appropriate way to behave in our culture, we should see this view incorporated into all aspects of life and thought. There seem to be four major sex-typed messages for males and females in our culture that have direct or indirect consequences on the way each sex may view death and may express those views. Table 3.1 presents these four stereotypic attitudes in a short form. The first major category for men is called the "stiff upper lip" syndrome. It embodies the need to be independent and self-sufficient (suggested by Brannon and discussed in Chapter 2) but goes beyond that. It encourages males to be less expressive than females in all areas of their internal lives, including their physical health and their feelings concerning death. Waldron (5) suggests that traditional men in our culture may ignore minor somatic complaints and not seek rest or care because it's not manly to be a cry baby. Goldberg (6) goes even further and proposes that part of a male's gender identity is to deny his body needs and to regard weakness as feminine. Thus, everyone's hero in high school is the football player who will continue to play in spite of painful injuries.

TABLE 3.1   Stereotypic Attitudes

Male	Female
Unexpressive, "stiff upper lip"	Anxious, hysteric
Powerful loner	Clinging vine
Provider	Nurturer
Macho man	Fragile, ultrafeminine

The analogous stereotype learned by women is that of
anxiety and hysteria. While a man in our culture is
taught not to focus on body needs, a woman is taught
early that her body is one of her most important assets.
She engages in body monitoring much earlier than does
her male peer. She also learns that it's all right,
perhaps even expected of her, to air her complaints and
symptoms. Statistics on the higher rates of women who
go to doctors and mental health centers seem to support
the fact that men, while they are at higher risk for
disease and death at every age, are more reluctant to
seek health care. Men make 25 percent fewer visits per
year to doctors and dentists, for example. However,
when they do go into the hospital, they stay an average
of 15 percent longer than do females (6). Perhaps these
statistics support the notion that males postpone admitting physical problems until it requires longer and more
detailed medical treatment than would be the case if
they had sought treatment earlier. In keeping with the
stiff upper lip syndrome, we might predict that males
would be less willing to admit death anxiety than
females and less willing to discuss personal fears.
Females, on the other hand, should be more willing to
share fears and anxieties about death from an early age
on in keeping with their learned role values, which permit admission of feelings and accept much higher levels
of affective behaviors, even approaching hysteria.

The second set of stereotypes that seems to have implications for male/female sex-differentiated attitudes toward
death includes the powerful loner for males and the
clinging vine stereotype for females. The powerful loner
stereotype may be related to higher male suicide rates
across the life span. Part of the traditional male socialization in our society seems to be a press toward distancing oneself from other people, in order to appear
rational and in control at all times. This type of
distancing results in an inability to express need even
in very stressful life circumstances. Women, on the
other hand, may display dependency needs in everyday
situations as well as in crisis situations without being
regarded as "out of role." Indeed, the very essence of
the clinging vine is her dependency on the stronger male.
She may feed into his stereotypic distancing behavior by
expecting him to be strong and silent at all times. Her
needs for support and direction from him may be so great
that she never discovers her own identity or individuality
for herself.

Support for the suggestion that this set of stereotypes
is still powerful in shaping behavior in our culture can
be found in statistics on divorce. Divorced and separated
women seek help in outpatient mental health facilities
at a rate 12 percent higher than do men. Divorced

and separated men, on the other hand outnumber women
in mental health institutions by 20 percent.

If you assume that institutionalization reflects more
severe pathology than outpatient treatment, you might
conclude that there is some support for the powerful
loner stereotype that prevents communication even in times
of stress. Add to this the fact that statistics show
the death rate for divorced males to be 3.16 times the
rate for divorced females, and you begin to see a
pretty convincing picture (6). Males who buy into this
stereotype would literally rather die than admit to
another human being that they cannot cope. Death anxiety
for this type of male would have to be denied or repressed, while the female opposite could be the very
personification of dependency in the face of death or
the threat of death.

The third general category of stereotypes is the one
that is most central to male/female identity. It is
the category of provider and nurturer, respectively.
In spite of women's mass entry into the labor
force, men in our culture are still viewed as the major
providers. Indeed, much of their worth is judged by the
quantity and quality of the bacon they bring home. Women,
on the other hand, are expected to put the nurturing of
others before their commitment to a job. They may leave
the labor force for a number of years to nurture young
children or, if economics permit, they may remain full-
time housewives and mothers throughout their adult lives
and never receive mass societal disapproval.

This is not true for the male, however. Even those males
who inherit wealth are expected to enter the family
business or choose a vocation. Otherwise, they are
regarded as playboys, not to be taken seriously. Those
men who are not wealthy and choose not to work are
regarded by society at large as bums, wastrels, or
parasites. So much of the male identity is tied up in
this provider role that the thought of illness and death
may be experienced as more severely threatening by males
than by females. Constant pressure on males from an
early age to provide for others may be related to the
higher incidence of Type A behavior experienced by men
and discussed in Chapter 2. If Selye is correct in his
assertion that "chronic disease mortality is caused by
the depletion of 'adaptation energy' primarily through
the operation of stress" (7), then defining a successful
man through the quality of his providing for others may
be inviting early death for that man.

The final stereotypes traditionally expected of males
and females are those of the macho man and the fragile,
ultrafeminine woman. The macho man, building on the
idea that competition is at the heart of the male role,

tries to outdo all comers in all types of behavior. He
pits himself against nature in a competition often to the
death in such overt risk-taking behaviors as sky diving,
playing chicken in cars, and motorcycle racing. He pits
his body against natural biological consequences by
indulging in smoking and excessive drinking. Men who
incorporate this stereotype into their attitudes of what
constitutes masculinity are uncomfortable with passivity
and have a real need to dominate every situation. Even
when they take up a leisure time fitness activity such
as tennis or running, they compete with their opponents
or against their own past record with a ferocity that
belies the concept of leisure and fitness. These men
frequently are the ones who can outsmoke, outdrink, out-
chew anyone and everyone and they may very well be the
ones who will develop the lung cancer, emphysema, cirrhosis of the liver, and heart disease to prove it.
Women who ascribe to the fragile, ultrafeminine stereotype may equate femininity with ill health and find
themselves making unnecessary visits to doctors and
being labeled by others as hypochondriacs. In their
youth, ultrafeminine women may enjoy an image of the
young, romantic heroine. However, as they age they may
find themselves being criticized for dressing too youth-
fully or failing to age gracefully. Some women invest
so much of their energy in this stereotype that they
come to believe life is not worth living if they cannot
maintain the ultrafeminine, fragile, romantic image of
their youth. The suicides, intentioned or subintentioned,
of such stars as Marilyn Monroe and Judy Garland, attest
to the fact that this stereotype has a limited useful
time span as well as to the fact that once incorporated
as a central facet of the identity, this stereotype is
powerful and compelling.

In summary, the four contrasting stereotypes that seem
to be central to differential gender identity may predispose males and females to differential rates of and
attitudes toward death. By examining the central
messages of the stereotypes, one might predict that males
will die more frequently at every age than females and
that females will be freer to admit anxiety and fear of
death than will males. One might also predict from the
provider stereotype that married men with families might
dread death more than would single men, and that males
and females would tend to grow more alike in death attitudes and death anxiety as they age and become less
dominated by stereotypical gender role presses.

SEX DIFFERENCES IN DEATH AND DEATH-RELATED CONCERNS
ACROSS THE LIFE SPAN

Having examined four messages that seem to be opposite for
males and females but that also seem to be central to the

identity of many individuals, we are in a position now to
examine the evidence concerning male and female attitudes
toward death and death-related concerns across the life
span. As we begin to look at representative literature,
we must be aware of general problems in the research on
this topic. Studies directed at observing sex differences
in death and death-related concerns are relatively rare.
Most of the studies we have on the topic of death do not
include analysis by sex. Sometimes they do not even
describe the sex of the subjects. Frequently they use
only one sex, although they may generalize their findings
to both sexes. Sometimes a sex difference is reported as
a secondary finding in research not originally set up to
examine this aspect. Such research is frequently very
weak methodologically. Having noted the problems in
this area of research, let us examine major findings concerning sex differentials in death and death-related
concerns by age periods across the life span.

Infancy and Childhood

The type of information that is available with respect
to infant mortality falls into two categories: first,
statistics on fetal and neonatal deaths and second,
articles on the dying infant, sudden infant death syndrome,
etc., most of which tend to look at the parents' reaction
to the terminally ill infant or to the sudden loss
child. The only sex differentials generally reported
during this period are those that are involved in the
death rate. In 1981, out of every 100,000 males under
the age of 12 months, there were 1,345 deaths compared
to 1,029 deaths for females. Table 3.2 shows the sex
differential in death in infancy and childhood and
supports the statement made in Chapter 2 that males
are at more risk than females at all ages in the life
span. Because of the higher frequency of death in
males, the sex ratio which was approximately 105 males
to 100 females at birth is reversed between the ages of
20 and 24. From that time on, women outnumber men in
the population and at an increasing rate. The largest
number of male to female deaths seems to occur just
after puberty (8).

Because infants are too young to be able to display
much understanding of death, it is logical that we were
not able to find any studies examining sex differences
in death concepts during the first two years. We did,
however, find studies dealing with parental and grand-
parental responses to infant death (9-12). One of the
central messages of these studies was the suggestion
that men have a more difficult time admitting loss and
coping with grief if they have been socialized to believe
in male competence and in the denial of feelings. Many
males seem to believe that the death of a child or grand-

TABLE 3.2   Expected Deaths per 1,000 Alive at Specified
Age, 1979

| Age in | White | | Black | |
| 1979 | | | | |
(years)	Male	Female	Male	Female
At birth	12.90	10.00	23.84	19.98
1	.93	.69	1.29	1.15
2	.68	.54	1.08	.95
3	.53	.44	.91	.77
4	.45	.36	.77	.62
5	.41	.30	.66	.49
6	.38	.27	.57	.40
7	.36	.24	.50	.32
8	.32	.21	.43	.27
9	.27	.19	.38	.24
10	.22	.18	.35	.23
11	.22	.18	.35	.23
12	.29	.20	.40	.25

Source: Statistical Abstract of the United States, 103d ed.,
1982-83. Washington, D.C.: U. S. Bureau of the Census, 1982, p. 72.

child is a failure in some way and somehow throws their
competence into question, or they act as though admitting
deep feelings of loss and grief would be showing weakness,
thus violating the stiff upper lip stereotype discussed
earlier.

Moving from infant mortality into the area of children
and death, we find an increase in both the number and
the general scope of articles available. The major
thrust of research on the subject of death with children
has been cognitive in nature. Accepting the Piagetian
notion that cognitive development follows a predictable
sequence related to both age and experience, many
researchers have shown that children attain mastery of
the concept of death in a gradual manner (13-20). Wass
(21) documents the general progression of cognitive
development as illustrated in Table 3.3 and relates it
to the acquisition of the concept of death. As we have
seen, children in the sensorimotor period, which is con-
comitant with infancy, are rarely studied concerning their
concept of death since they are so limited in their
ability to express themselves. However, anecdotal
evidence exists that 2-year-olds are able to differentiate
life and living from the state of death. Kastenbaum (22),
for example, tells the story of a 16-month-old who clearly
recognizes the difference between the states of life and

TABLE 3.3 Development of Death Concepts

Predominant Death Concepts	Piaget's Period/State of Cognitive Development	Life Period
1. No concept of death	Sensorimotor period	Infancy
2. Death is reversible: a temporary restriction, departure, or sleep	Stage of preoperational thought	Late infancy Early childhood
3. Death is irreversible but capricious; external-internal physiological explanations	Stage of concrete operations	Middle childhood; late childhood or preadolescence
4. Death is irreversible, universal, personal, but distant; natural, physiological and theological explanations.	Period of formal operations	Preadolescence Adolescence Adulthood

Source: Wass (21).

death. The scene he describes is a garden where the young child is watching a caterpillar make its way along the path.

> The child notices the approach of big adult feet moving along the path. He shows an alarmed expression, according to his companion, a senior biomedical scientist who is also the boy's father. In a moment the caterpillar lies crushed. The boy bends over the remains, studying them intently. Finally, he stands up and announces in a sad and re-. signed voice, "No more." (p. 114)

It may well be that recognition of the alive and active state is one of the human being's first acquired concepts. It is certainly true that the relative ignorance concerning what the word dead means begins to give way between the ages of 3 and 4. Children at this age tend to recognize the word "death" and to associate it with coffins, graves and graveyards, a sleep-like condition, hospitals, and so on. They still, however, seem to regard death as a transitory, reversible, and far from universal state. One study of 3- and 5-year-olds found class and age differences in death awareness. However, it found no sex differences in the awareness of the concepts of universality, irreversibility, causality, and fear of death in the sample (23).

Around the age of 5 or 6, children pass from the pre-operational stage of thought into concrete operations and begin to get a firm grasp on the idea of irreversibility in death as in other concepts. They also begin to explore cause-effect relations during this period and can thus give specific and real explanations of what occurs to bring about death. In one study, all children by the age of 9 recognized that death was a universal event (24); that all people born must die. Also during the concrete operations stage, many children become fascinated with the physical details surrounding death-- embalming, funerals, etc. Through this curiosity, children begin to develop the idea that death is a natural, even necessary event. They still often protect themselves from death anxiety by viewing death as something that happens only to the elderly or will occur to them only after a great deal of time has passed. Wass and Scott (25) quote a 12-year-old boy as saying:

> Well, to me death is a natural thing. Every-
> body has to die sometime. Nobody lives for-
> ever. I know that my mother and father will
> die sometime. I just hope it's not soon.
> Then, later, I myself will be threatened by
> this natural thing called death. (p. 11)

Around age 11 or 12, children begin to develop formal operations, which are the most advanced stage of cognitive development, according to Piaget. With regard to death, this usually means that children can fully understand that death is universal, unavoidable, natural, irreversible and that it is a real personal event that will happen to them.

Before we leave our discussion of the development of the concept of death, we should note that different children pass through this sequence at different rates. There is some evidence that exposure to death speeds up understanding of the meaning of death (26). The question of whether consistent sex differences in understanding death occur at this time is still unresolved, since most articles dealing with children in the concrete operations stage did not examine sex differences. Perhaps because they were frequently operating from a Piagetian framework and Piaget did not find sex differences in cognitive development, the researchers assumed that no sex differences in death would be found. Of 41 articles reviewed in the area of

infancy and childhood, only eight seemed to have examined
their data for sex differences. Of the eight, three
articles found no sex differences while five reported
differences in some aspects of death awareness.

One study (27) reported that by the time children
reached the sixth grade (approximately 11 years of age)
the boys have begun to evidence some of the denial predicted by the socialization stereotypes previously
mentioned. The boys, compared to the girls in the study,
indicated much lowered incidences of frightening dreams
and were significantly less likely to admit fears at
bedtime. Unwillingness to express fear or weakness may
lead to inability to face death either in the abstract
or when faced with a personal instance of it. Another
report (28) shows that among males who were institutionalized and diagnosed as highly depressed, 37.8 percent
had lost a parent before age 16. The corresponding
figure for women in the highly depressed group was 25.4
percent. Since depression, at least at this time in our
culture, tends to be more common among women in the general population, the results of this study may support
the allegation that traditional male sex role socialization may more negatively affect male children's ability
to cope with death. Three studies conducted in the 1970s
looked at children and suicide. One of these (29) studied
34 severely depressed children under 12 years of age who
were self-abusive and/or suicidal. Of this population,
23 were males and 11 were females. The authors point out
that the 2-to-1 ratio of males to females affirms earlier
documented sex-difference incidence rates in suicide.
No significant difference was found in the ideational
violence between boys and girls. A second reference on
the subject of children and suicide notes that in
Britain more boys than girls committed suicide and that,
like adults, the boys tended to use highly lethal methods
including shooting and hanging while the girls were more
likely to take overdoses of drugs or to use gas (30).
A third reference on suicide seems to support in essence
the findings of the other two in that it points out that
the risk of suicide is very high in the 15- to 25-year-
old age group, especially for males (31). Perhaps male
socialization for competence increases the likelihood of
successful suicide. We will be examining suicide in the
general population more closely in Chapter 4.

Summary. The data on sex differences in death in infancy
and childhood are far from clear. Preliminary findings,
based often on weak or unreplicated research, may support
the notion that females do admit fear and anxiety with
greater freedom by around age 10 or 11, which is the same
time as realization of the full meaning of death becomes
stabilized. The research also shows that while boys may
be more reluctant to admit fear of weakness, they are
more likely than girls to commit suicide and to do so
utilizing more violent means.

TABLE 3.4   Excess Percentages of Male to Female Deaths

Cause of Death	%
Accidents	74
Suicide	75
Malignant neoplasms	37
Heart disease	45
Pneumonia	13
Cerebrovascular diseases	12

Source: U.S. National Center for Health Statistics, 1978.

Adolescence and Young Adulthood

Moving to the age of adolescence and young adulthood, we find that much more information on death and death-related concerns is available. Although adolescence is the period when general health and strength peak, there is still a sex differential in the incidence of death. For example, of the total male deaths reported in 1981, 16 percent were adolescent males. The comparable figure for female adolescents is 7 percent of the total deaths of women. Six major causes of death, in particular, reveal inequities between the sexes.

Table 3.4 shows clearly that even during the healthy period of adolescence, males are more at risk of death than are females. It is particularly telling then to note that studies measuring death anxiety in the 15- to 25-year-olds tend to support the idea that females show significantly higher death anxiety than do males (32-34). In addition, the death anxiety of adolescents seems to resemble that of their parents, at least in early adolescence (35, 36). Females tend to resemble their mothers but not their fathers in fear of death. Males tend to move closer to their parents in fear of death as they move through adolescence, while females tend to resemble their parents less as time goes by (37).

Males and females during adolescence and early adulthood seem to emphasize different aspects of death. Both sexes seem to associate death more frequently with males, perhaps as a recognition of the higher death incidence in males (38). However, females tend to emphasize loss when reacting to death themes while males emphasize violence and destruction. Males also have been found to favor killing in war more than do females (39). In addition, females reported viewing death as a peaceful and religious experience more frequently than did males (40). Females seem also to be more likely to think

TABLE 3.5   Percent of Increase in Suicide by Sex and
Age, 1961-1975

Sex	Age	%
Males	15-19	130
Females	15-19	93
Males	20-24	138
Females	20-24	113

Source: Holinger, P.V.   Adolescent suicide: An epidemiological
study of recent trends.   American Journal of Psychiatry, 1978,
135, 6.

about dying from a specific disease, to wish they were
dead, to report becoming depressed by funerals and
cemeteries, and to believe in life after death than do
males (41).   Among young adults, two studies have shown
that people who scored higher on measures of self-actual-
ization also reported lower death anxiety (42, 43).   The
question of suicide in adolescence will be reviewed in
detail in the next chapter.   Suffice it to say here that
suicide has reached epidemic proportions among adolescents
and young adults in the United States.   Holinger (44)
points out that suicide rates increased 131% in the 15-
to 24-year-old age group between 1961 and 1975.   Once
again the number of male to female suicides creates a
now familiar pattern, as revealed in Table 3.5.   Males
are also at higher risk for death by accident.   Accidents
are the leading cause of death during this period, and
many of these may be disguised or subintentioned suicides
(45).

Summary.   Sex differences do seem to be evident in death
and death-related concerns during adolescence and young
childhood.   Males seem to deny death anxiety more frequently than do females.   Females tend to admit anxiety
and fear but also paradoxically tend to view death as
more peaceful and less violent than do males.   Females
also tend to admit more depressive and religious feelings
when confronted with death and death-related concerns
than do males.   Males, however, while not reporting
depression concerning death as frequently as do ·females,
tend to commit suicide more frequently and to be involved
in accidents more frequently than females.   While the
causes for the differential rates of death are far from
clear, it may be hypothesized that females have "less
to prove" and are freer to admit concerns, fears, and
weaknesses than are males at this time.

TABLE 3.6   Death Rates, by Cause, Sex and Age, 1979

Sex and Age	Diseases of Heart	Malignant Neoplasms	Cerebro-vascular Diseases	Acci-dents	Pneu-monia, Flu
U.S.	333.1	183.3	77.0	47.8	20.5
Male	370.4	205.6	65.8	69.5	22.2
25-44 yr	36.1	26.2	5.6	70.4	2.9
45-64 yr	516.0	345.6	52.8	63.2	16.0
65 yr and over	2,751.7	1,364.3	571.8	126.6	184.0
Female	297.9	162.1	87.6	27.3	18.8
25-44 yr	12.4	30.2	5.1	17.6	1.6
45-64 yr	178.4	266.7	41.8	22.1	7.7
65 yr and over	1,989.5	759.9	598.4	77.5	124.1

Source on following page

Maturity

The period of adulthood, starting in the mid-twenties and ending around age 65, is one for which there is a dearth of any type of research for our purposes.

The major hard data available for adults are the figures that show the continuing sex differential in the incidence of death. Table 3.6 shows the death rates by cause, sex, and age per 100,000 mature residents during 1979. When the data are summed across the middle years, it is apparent that males die more frequently than females in every category.

Until very recently, anyone viewing the research available across the life span would have been forced to conclude that childhood and adolescence represented interesting periods for the study of change and development, and that old age was interesting in its research implications, but that the period of adulthood must be a boring one indeed. One tongue-in-cheek account (46) has described middle age in the following manner:

> Middle age is the wasteland between adolescence and senescence. It is nature's way of yawning between one important job--getting us grown up--and another one--getting us out of the way. Yes, occasionally something does happen between youth and old age that you might call maturity. We come across all kinds of unusual phenomena in biology, zoology, and

TABLE 3.6   Death Rates, by Cause, Sex and Age, 1979, Cont'd

Sex and Age	Diabetes Mellitus	Cirrhosis of Liver	Arterio- sclerosis	Suicide	Early Infancy Diseases
U.S.	15.1	13.5	13.1	12.4	10.7
Male	12.9	18.1	10.7	18.9	12.5
25-44 yr	2.7	10.9	.1	24.4	(x)
45-64 yr	17.9	50.0	3.7	23.9	(x)
65 yr and over	91.0	55.2	105.9	36.7	(x)
Female	17.2	9.2	15.4	6.1	8.9
25-44 yr	2.0	4.9	-	8.4	(x)
45-64 yr	16.8	23.5	1.9	10.2	(x)
65 yr and over	101.3	23.4	115.5	7.0	(x)

Source: Statistical abstract of the U.S., 1982-83, 103d edition, p. 77. Washington D.C.: U.S. Bureau of the Census, 1982.

> medicine. But for most men and women, the middle years make up a prolonged interval of deadening routine....Youth is the dawning generation. We, the middle-aged, are the yawning generation... (p. 543)

Opposing the idea that after the turbulence of adolescence there comes a relatively stable and even boring period of life are those researchers who have given America a new term: the mid-life crisis. At least three researchers (47-49) have independently documented a transitional stage that many men seem to experience during the early part of the decade of the forties (there were no women included in these three studies). Although limited in generalizability because their populations were largely middle-class white males, these studies do document a shift in the thinking of adults that is relevant to the study of attitudes toward death. Levinson and his colleagues (47), for example, describe mid-life as a time when individuals need to confront their own mortality and overcome earlier illusions of omnipotence. Gould (48) speaks of a growing tendency in mid-life to consider the existential questions of "self, values and life itself..." (p. 526). He also speaks of a sense of "quiet desperation and an increasing awareness of time squeeze" (p. 526). Vaillant and McArthur report an increase in depression accompanying an often agonizing reevaluation of life goals with an eye to time remaining (49). In short, at least for some people, middle age seems to be a time in which the meaning of death to life

becomes a central issue. A shift in the sense of time
from time since birth to time remaining until death has
been documented. The realization that time remaining is
finite, that there will not be enough time to accomplish
all we might wish, is perhaps one of the leading causes
of the turbulence that makes up the mid-life crisis.

One study is available, however, which was designed
specifically to examine the relationships among mid-life
transition, death anxiety, and self actualization (50).
Subjects were university faculty members between the
ages of 27 and 55, who were assigned to premid-life,
mid-life, and postmid-life groups. The mid-life transition group scored significantly higher in death anxiety
than the other two groups, thus supporting the concept
that death and the amount of time left to live are
central issues in mid-life. Not surprisingly, sex
differences were not included as a focus of this study.

Sex differences in death anxiety and views of death,
however, have been documented among this age group.
At least six studies have attempted to examine adults
of different ages with respect to some aspect of death
anxiety. One study (referred to previously as adolescents
were included in the sample) is that of Templer, Russ,
and Franks (36). They studied five diverse groups
ranging in age from 13 to 85. They found no correlation
between age and death anxiety but found that females
scored significantly higher in death anxiety in every
group than did males. Berman and Hays (51) also found
that females were higher in death anxiety as well as in
belief in afterlife. These researchers also found support for the idea that fear of death decreases as a
result of higher levels of education. A third study
(52) found that females had higher death anxiety than
did males, while no correlation was found between
religion or risk-taking behavior and death anxiety. A
fourth researcher, however, found that religious ortho-
doxy worked against males viewing death as "sadness"
(53). The more religious a male was, the more likely he
was to regard death as "peaceful bliss." Females,
however, regardless of religiosity, tended to see death
as sadness. The author concluded that "women may be
more homogeneous in their conceptions of death than are
men" (p. 110). Chiappetta and associates (32) not only
found that females had higher death anxiety than did
males, but also found that females tended to cope with
this anxiety by cognitively manipulating death-related
variables more effectively than did males. A sixth
study, which utilized subjects between the ages of 45
and 75, also looked at three ethnic groups: Blacks,
Mexican-Americans, and Anglos. In the overall analysis,
men showed less fear of death. The middle-aged group,
ages 45-54, expressed more fear of death than did the
other age groups. The older age group, 55-64, reported

thinking about death more frequently. The lowest fear
of death was found among older black men (54). The
authors conclude that this study supports the middle-aged
crisis--evidenced by many persons confronting death--as
well as the apparent resolution of the crisis by the
elderly. They suggest that age may be a "leveler of
prior social distinctions, as aging individuals from
various social categories deal with the inevitability of
impending death" (p. 76). Sex differences in this research approached, but did not reach, statistical
significance, with females expressing greater fears
than did males.

Two studies attempted to examine the relationship of
marital status to death and death anxiety. The first,
done by Gove (55), dealt only with whites between the
ages of 25 and 64. He found that single men were twice
as likely to commit suicide as married men, while single
women were only 51 percent more likely than married
women to commit suicide. For men, the shift from being
single to being married decreased their likelihood of
being murdered, while for women the reverse was true.
In the area of accidents and disease, the single statuses
again seem to be more dangerous for men than for women.
Gove's conclusions bear repeating:

> In all cases, the shift from being single to
> being married appears, from the mortality rates,
> to have a more favorable effect on men than on
> women, while the shift from the married to an
> unmarried state appears to have a more unfavor-
> able effect on men than on women. For men
> being unmarried is uniformly associated with
> mortality rates that are higher than those of
> the married, with the widowed and divorced
> having especially high rates. The data for
> women are generally similar, although the re-
> lationships are neither as strong nor as
> consistent. (pp. 52-53)

Gove believed that marital roles, closely based on sex
role socialization, account for the differences between
the sexes.

The second study set out to explore the effect that the
male's role as provider had on death anxiety (56).
Subjects were 150 residents of a southeastern community:
79 males and 71 females. The author of the study hypothesized that married men with children would have the
highest death anxiety, followed by childless married
men, and that both categories of married men would have
higher death anxiety than married women. None of his
hypotheses was supported. The only significant difference
he found was between death anxiety levels in single males

and single females, with single males atypically scoring
higher in death anxiety than single females.

Summary. The mature years, from 25-64, are the least
researched period of the life span. In the area of
death, we find that the sex differential increases so
that females outnumber males in the population. We also
find a fairly clear picture regarding death anxiety,
with females, especially in the younger ages, admitting
more death anxiety than do males. Somewhere in the
decade of the forties, there is evidence that a mid-life
crisis is experienced by some. One of the central
issues in this crisis involves a reexamination of
earlier dreams, priorities, and values in the face of
the acute awareness of the finiteness of time and the
inevitability of death. Studies done with people toward
the end of this age period seem to indicate that both
males and females who have successfully resolved the
mid-life crisis experience less death anxiety. This
latter finding may provide support for those who say
that sex role distinctions in general become less pro-
nounced after mid-life.

The Older Years

Research on death and death-related concerns among the
elderly is plentiful. In addition, because this is the
period of life in which widowhood is statistically very
likely to occur, much of the research on death with this
age group has been done with those who have been widowed.
Chapter 5 will be dealing with loss, so the studies on
widowhood will not be included in this section. Before
we begin this section, however, we should note that
discussions of the elderly are often misleading. As is
true of the "middle-aged," studies done with the elderly
tend to lump together people over a large age range
without regard to their differences. Not only are there
great differences in physiological functioning between
the average 65-year-old and the average 90-year-old, but
there are also cohort differences and large individual
differences in personality. Contrary to popular belief,
the elderly tend to be more different than any segment
of the population, at least until death is imminent.
The reason for this is that the elderly have had more
years to increase their individual differences and to
build their own unique life histories. Human beings are
more alike at birth than they will ever be again.
Differences increase proportionately to the amount of
time lived since birth, as individuals are constantly
building their own singular identities. Therefore, it
should not be surprising to find contradictions in the
literature. Wass and her colleagues, stressing the
great differences among the elderly, reviewed literature
that showed that "fear of death in old people varies

with a number of factors and conditions such as physical
health status, psychological health, and degree of social
distance among others" (57, p. 339).

As with other age groups discussed, it is not within the
scope of this section to review every study undertaken
on the subject of death and the elderly. Rather, it is
our intention to review those studies which shed light
on characteristics and attitudes of the elderly population regarding death with special attention to the sex
differential in death and death-related attitudes.

It has been said that the young may face death while
the old must face death. During the aged period of
life we reach 100 percent mortality. No elderly person
survives old age. However, even during this period
we can observe sex differences. In 1970, the elderly
comprised about 10 percent of the total population;
by the year 2010, between 13 and 15 percent of the
population will be over 65. Currently, there are more
than 135 women to every 100 men over age 65 in the
United States, and this ratio increases with age from
120/100 at ages 65-69 to over 160/100 at age 85 and
older (58). It is during this period that we see the
culmination of earlier trends in death rates. The
male death rate exceeds that of the female in six of
the nine major causes of death among the elderly, as
revealed in Table 3.7.

Especially in the current elderly cohort, life-style
differences may be affecting the differential rates.
Our older population today disapproved more of women
using alcohol and cigarettes than it did of their use
by men. These cultural prescriptions may still be
providing some protection for women against death from
cirrhosis, cancer, heart disease, and pneumonia. Once
again the male sex role may be implicated in the differential figures, as we saw at the beginning of this
chapter.

Common wisdom states that older people fear death less
than do younger people. Perhaps underlying this belief
is the knowledge that the elderly have experienced a
life history, that they have had time to achieve that
which they were capable of doing, and therefore death
becomes less of a loss to them. Additionally, quality
of life issues may feed into common wisdom. As people
age, they inevitably experience loss of bodily functioning, of friends and of desires, thus perhaps decreasing
their joy in existence. In short, the elderly may have
more reasons than the young to view death with less
fear; perhaps even to embrace it, depending on their
life circumstances.

TABLE 3.7   Death Rates by Cause, Sex, and Age, 1979[a]

Sex and Age	Diseases of Heart	Malignant Neoplasms	Cerebro-vascular Diseases	Acci-dents	Pneu-monia, Flu
U.S.A.	331.1	183.3	77.0	47.8	20.5
Male	370.4	205.6	65.8	69.5	22.2
65 and over	2,751.7	1,364.3	571.8	126.6	184.0
Female	297.9	162.1	87.6	27.3	18.8
65 and over	1,989.5	759.9	598.4	77.5	124.1

Footnote and source on following page.

Much of common wisdom has been borne out by research on death anxiety among the elderly. Templer found that older adults (aged 60-83) had significantly lower death anxiety scores than did younger adults (59). Kalish and Reynolds found that although the elderly had encountered significantly more death situations and had attended significantly more funerals than younger people in their sample, they showed less fear of death (60). The researchers concluded that "the aged are more accepting of death in general and their own death in particular than are younger persons" (p. 205). One interesting sex difference found in this study that was true of the elderly as well as of younger groups was that men desired to live longer than did women and denied the statistics concerning differential death rates by stating that they expected to live as long as did women. A study done by Moriya in Japan found a sex difference in desire to live to 100 expressed by younger people but not for older people, with a higher percentage of males than females wanting to live that long (61). Moriya concluded that "the sex difference in relative immortal desire tends to diminish as aging [sic]" (p. 42). This latter study seems to show that older people desire to live to a very old age less than do younger people and that males and females become more alike in their desire to live to an old age as they get older.

Several studies have found correlations between psychological factors and death concern or death anxiety among the aged. For example, Rhudick and Dibner (62) found that those who scored high on hypochondriasis, hysteria, dependency, and impulsivity on the MMPI had higher death

TABLE 3.7   Death Rates by Cause, Sex, and Age, 1979[a] (Cont'd)

Sex and Age	Diabetes Mellitus	Cirrhosis of Liver	Arterio-sclerosis	Suicide	Early Infancy Diseases
U.S.A.	15.1	13.5	13.1	12.4	10.7
Male 65 and	12.9	18.1	10.7	18.9	12.5
over	91.0	55.2	105.9	36.7	(x)
Female 65 and	17.2	9.2	15.4	6.1	8.9
over	101.3	23.4	115.5	7.0	(x)

[a](Rates per 100,000 estimated midyear population. Excludes non-residents of United States. Causes of death classified according to ninth revision of the International Classification of Diseases.)

Source: U.S. National Center for Health Statistics, Vital Statistics of the United States, Annual, 1978.

Statistical abstract of the U.S., 1982-83, 103d edition, p. 77. Washington, D.C.: U.S. Bureau of the Census, 1982.

concern scores. They found "no demonstrable relationship between type of death attitude and sex, age and occupational status" (p. 47). Keily and Dudek found significant differences between depressed and normal groups in terms of negative attitudes and feelings toward death. However, they also failed to find significant sex or ethnic group differences (63). Christ (64), Wolff (65), and Templer (59) have all shown that fear of death is higher among elderly who have severe emotional and personality disorders than among normal older people.

Other factors that have been researched in studies on death attitudes among the elderly include education level, socioeconomic level, health status, housing situation, activity level, and religious conviction. Lipman and Marden (66) found that people's ability to make preparation for their own deaths was affected by source of income, education, and race; once again sex did not seem to be a factor. These authors found that subjects who received part or all of their income from welfare showed less responsibility in death planning than those whose income was from other sources.

Support for sex differences in death attitudes among the
elderly has been found in at least two studies. Sanders,
Poole, and Rivero (67) studied a sample that included
62 black and white adults between the ages of 60 and 87
years. They found both black and white females had
higher death anxiety than did the males in the study.
They also found that, overall, male and female blacks
had higher mean death anxiety scores than did the
whites. Wass and Sisler (68) found that female elderly
persons had significantly higher death concern scores
than did males. They also found that rural elderly had
higher death concern than did small town or urban elderly.
High death concern scores were also correlated with low
income in this population and with widowed marital
status. The scores decreased as the frequency with
which subjects thought about their own deaths decreased.
Those people who were in good health and who reported
pleasure in being alive had lower death concern scores,
as did those indicating that mourning and grief rituals
were of little importance to bereaved people and that
they preferred cremation or were indifferent to the
method of disposal of their bodies. In summary, this
study seems to indicate that "demographic factors with
which high death concern scores were associated include
female sex, widowhood, solitary living, rural dwelling,
low education level, and low income" (p. 84). These
results complement the earlier study of Jeffers, Nichols,
and Eisdorfer (69), which found that factors associated
with no fear of death include "a tendency to read the
Bible oftener, more belief in a future life, reference
to death with more religious connotations, fewer feelings
of rejection and depression, higher scores on full scale
and performance IQ tests, and more responses on the
Rorschach (with the suggestion also of more leisure
activities)" (p. 54). Another older study, done by
Swenson, which found no significant relationship between
sex and death attitudes, did find support for religious
conviction and housing situation variables as important
factors in attitudes toward death (70). Swenson found
in his sample of 152 females and 58 males that persons
with "more fundamental religious convictions and habits
look forward to death more than do those with less
fundamental convictions and less (religious) activity.
Fearful attitudes toward death tend to be found in those
persons with little religious activity" (p. 54). The
importance of these older studies might be disregarded
since the cohort who was over 60 in the 1960s was surely
much different demographically than those who reached
60 in the late 1970s. However, since the Wass study
confirms these findings, it may be true that older co-
horts show differential death concern and/or anxiety as
a function of their religious beliefs and location of
residence. Swenson's study also showed that fear of
death was higher among those who lived alone, and that
those who were in good health were evasive about death

as were the less educated and the widowed in his sample;
those who were college graduates or were single, separated,
or married and those who were in poor health looked forward to death.   In a more recent study, Nehrke and his
associates found that death anxiety decreased as age of
his sample increased.   They described the older women
in their sample as "more externally controlled, lower
in life satisfaction, lower in years of schooling and
lower in death anxiety than the younger women..." (71,
p. 366).   They also found that life satisfaction was
significantly lower for nursing home residents than for
those living in public housing or in the general community.   Finally, Palmore and Stone (72) found four
significant predictors of longevity.   These included
physical mobility, education, occupation, and employment.
Since longevity is the obverse of dying, these factors
may well be important in any consideration of death and
the elderly.   Environmental factors such as relocation,
retirement, and the death of significant others have
also been shown in one study to affect death rates and
death attitudes of the elderly adversely.

One area of research interest with the elderly has been
that of psychological and cognitive change when death
is imminent.   A study done with 88 women over the age of
62 indicated that the elderly may protect themselves
from death anxiety by becoming less future oriented (73).
This study is complemented by one done by Moore and
Newton (74), which suggests that older people react to
the threat of dying with denial.   The authors found, in
a study of 29 patients--11 males and 18 females--that
the dying elderly, when compared to staff and family,
more frequently "denied concerns such as bodily suffering,
pain, changes in mental state, ..." (p. 135).   The
elderly dying were also unwilling to admit consideration
of their own death and to admit that death was a part of
life.

In the area of cognitive changes, recent research has
pointed to the existence of a terminal drop among those
who are dying.   As early as 1961, one researcher reported
observations of intellectual changes in an aged population approximately two years prior to their death (75).
This study was followed by one that essentially replicated
these observations (76).   In 1965 a study was done to
determine if systematic psychological changes occurred
prior to death in the very aged (77).   Using a sample
of 25 residents of a home for the aged, tests were
conducted over a two-and-a-half-year period.   The
researchers concluded that there were changes prior to
death within this sample.   The changes were described
as "a diminution of the capacity to cope adequately with
environmental demands, particularly because of a lowered
ability to organize and integrate stimuli in the environment" (p. 190).   Another study was reported that perform-

ance on tests of learning and retention as well as on
tests of time and space orientation decreased significantly
in subjects near death (78). In 1971, Riegel reported
cognitive change as measured by IQ tests of such magni-
tude that he believed that much of the age differences
between young and old subjects in cross-sectional
intelligence studies might be due to terminal drop (79).
Another group of researchers set out to develop a
battery of behavioral procedures which might be "predictors of ensuing death among the elderly" (80, p. 759).
The researchers administered a battery of 18 tasks to
380 healthy persons between 60 and 89 years of age.
Five years later they compared the scores of those still
living with those who had died. They found that 13 of
the 18 tasks proved to discriminate significantly when
age and sex were matched. Therefore, they found support
for the idea that cognitive functioning does change
among elderly prior to death. Another study of cognitive changes included an examination of differential
behavior by the sexes (81). The authors found support
for the concept of terminal drop in general. They
also described a finding which appears to be different
for the sexes. They found that the percentage of
female deaths for those who scored in the lower range
in IQ measures was very significantly higher than for
those who scored in the middle and upper ranges; for men,
the percentage of deaths among the lower ranges did not
reach statistical significance. This study may indicate
that cognitive changes preceding death are more severe
for females than for males. One final study related to
this area attempted to structure a death-concerns
cognitive domain (82). Utilizing males and females from
20 to 80 years of age, the author found that subjects
having high death anxiety tended toward ambivalence,
cognitive disorganization, and less consistency of
emotional response, with that tendency being more pro-
nounced for males. The results of this study might
suggest that death anxiety is a variable which feeds
into cognitive disorganization. Since death anxiety
may be exacerbated when death is imminent, it might
well feed into lower levels of cognitive functioning at
death. That the sexes should be examined separately
was underlined by this author when she said, "I suggest
that these results correspond to the cultural expectations
for emotional expression in both sexes. Males are expected
not to admit fear (i.e., show less avoidance content),
whereas females are allowed and even expected to admit
fear (i.e., show greater avoidance content). These
expectations for expression of affect are dictated by
cultural gender-role definitions: the males as assertive
and stoic, the female as dependent and 'emotional'"
(p. 180). It would seem that even in cognitive handling
of death, sex differences based on socialization may be
important variables to note.

Summary. There seems to be growing evidence that elderly people, compared with younger people, fear death less, perhaps in part because of the defense of denial. In addition, although contradictory studies do appear, the majority of the evidence seems to indicate that males and females still show different reactions to death and death-related concerns. Females seem freer to admit death anxiety or fear, while males may move in that direction but still tend to be less expressive. Factors of religiosity, place of residence, socioeconomic status, race, and intelligence all seem important in determining an elderly person's response to death. Cognitive functioning does seem to decrease prior to death. Since the elderly are more dissimilar than people at any other stage of life, future research in this area needs to be more finely grained as it attempts to identify variables important in male and female reactions to death.

SUMMARY AND CONCLUSIONS

We began this chapter by examining the components of attitudes: cognitive, affective, and behavioral. We then examined the basic way in which gender identity and gender roles with their accompanying attitudes are formed. We suggested four bi-polar stereotypes that characterize extreme traditional sex role socialization. We then predicted on the basis of the stereotypes that men in the general population would have higher mortality rates, would admit less death anxiety, and might show differential levels of death anxiety based on marital and parenting status.

Although some literature for each age group is contra-dictory and incomplete, some basic conclusions appear to be emerging regarding sex differences in death and death-related concerns across the life span. The first is the clear statistical evidence that men die at higher rates in all ages. Since suicide and accidents are major factors in the higher death rates of males from adolescence on, and since some of the other major diseases (e.g., cirrhosis of the liver, pneumonia, and other lung diseases) may reflect discrepant socialization pressures, it seems fair to conclude that male gender role socialization is one major factor in the sex differential in death. Furthermore, single males seem to be at higher risk than married males for almost every cause of death.

The literature seems to support the contention that females report higher death anxiety than do males, particularly through middle adulthood. The evidence for greater female fear of death is less conclusive during old age. These findings may be interpreted as support for the general contention that sex role impera-

tives for males and females begin to lessen. No support
was found for the contention that male marital and
parenting status affects death anxiety.

Other factors which have been shown to be related to
death attitudes at the various ages were discussed.
Some of these factors include intelligence, past
experience with death, widowhood, mental health status,
educational level, socioeconomic status, race, place of
residence, and religiosity.

REFERENCES

1. Hoyenga, K. B., & Hoyenga, K. T. The question of
   sex differences. Boston: Little, Brown, 1979.

2. Kohlberg, L., & Ullman, O. Z. Stages in the
   development of psychosexual concepts and attitudes.
   In R. C. Friedman, R. M. Richart, and R. L. Vande
   Wiele (Eds.), Sex differences in behavior (pp. 209-
   222). New York: Wiley, 1974.

3. Master, J. C., & Wilkinson, A. Consensual and
   discriminative stereotypes of sex-type judgments by
   parents and children. Child Development, 1976, 47,
   208-217.

4. Rebecca, M., Hefner, & Oleshansky, B. A model
   of sex-role transcendence. Journal of Social
   Issues, 1976, 32, 197-206.

5. Waldron, I. Why do men live longer than women?
   Social Science and Medicine, 1976, 10, 349-362.

6. Goldberg, H. The hazards of being male: Surviving
   the myth of masculine privilege. New York: Signet,
   New American Library, 1977.

7. Selye, H. The stress of life. New York: McGraw-
   Hill, 1956.

8. Childs, B. Genetic origin of some sex differences
   among human beings. Pediatrics, 1965, 35, 798-812.

9. Carney, R. T., & Horton, F. T., Jr. Pathological
   grief following spontaneous abortion. American
   Journal of Psychiatry, 1974, 131, 825-827.

10. Gyulay, J. The forgotten grievers. American Journal
    of Nursing, 1975, 75, 1476-1479.

11. Kennell, J. The mourning response of parents to
    the death of a newborn infant. The New England
    Journal of Medicine, 1970, 283, 344-349.

12. Seitz, P., & Warrick, L. H. et al. Perinatal death. American Journal of Nursing, 1974, 74, 2028-2033.

13. Childers, P., & Wimmer, M. The concept of death in early childhood. Child Development, 1971, 42, 1299-1301.

14. Gartley, W., & Bernasconi, M. The concept of death in children. Journal of Genetic Psychology, 1967, 110, 71-85.

15. Hansen, Y. Development of the concept of death: Cognitive aspects. General Psychology, 1972, 640, 152.

16. Kane, B. Children's concept of death. Journal of Genetic Psychology, 1979, 134, 141-153.

17. Koocher, G. Talking with children about death. American Journal of Orthopsychiatry, 1974, 44, 404-411.

18. Melear, J. Children's conceptions of death. Journal of Genetic Psychology, 1973, 123, 359-360.

19. Nagy, M. The child's theories concerning death. Journal of Genetic Psychology, 1948, 73, 3-27.

20. Tallmer, M., Formanek, R., & Tallmer, T. Factors influencing children's concepts of death. Journal of Clinical Child Psychology, 1974, 3(2), 17-19.

21. Wass, H. Concepts of death: A developmental perspective. In H. Wass & C. A. Corr, (Eds.), Childhood and death. Washington: Hemisphere, 1984.

22. Kastenbaum, R. Death, society and human experience, St. Louis: Mosby, 1977.

23. Beauchamp, N. The young child's perception of death. Dissertation Abstracts International, Dec. 1974, 35, 3288-3239.

24. Bolduc, J. A developmental study of the relationship between experiences of death and age and development of the concept of death. Dissertation Abstracts International, 1972.

25. Wass, H., & Scott, M. Middle school students' death concepts and concerns. Middle School Journal, 1978, 9, 10-12.

26. Bluebond-Langner. The private world of dying children. Princeton, N.J.: University Press, 1978.

27. Bauer, D. An exploratory study of developmental
     changes in children's fears. Journal of Child
     Psychiatry, 1976, 17, 69-74.

28. Beck, A. T., Sethi, B. B., & Tuthill, R. W. Child-
     hood bereavement and adult depression. Archives
     of General Psychiatry, 1963, 9, 295-336.

29. Paulson, M. J., Stone, D., Spasto, R., & Paulson,
     A. Suicide potential and behavior in children
     ages 4 to 12. Suicide and Life Threatening
     Behavior, 1978, 4(8), 225-242.

30. Suicide in children (unauthored review). British
     Medical Journal, 1975, N5958, 592.

31. Renshaw, D. Suicide and depression in children.
     Journal of School Health, 1974, 44(9), 487-489.

32. Chiappetta, W., Floyd, H., & McSeveney, D. R. Sex
     differences in coping with death anxiety. Psycho-
     logical Reports, 1976, 39, 945-946.

33. Iammarino, N. Relationship between death anxiety
     and demographic variables. Psychological Reports,
     1975, 37, 262.

34. Thorson, J. A. Variations in death anxiety related
     to college students' sex, major field of study, and
     certain personality traits. Psychological Reports,
     1977, 40, 857-858.

35. Lester, D. Relation of fear of death in subjects
     to fear of death in their parents. Psychological
     Reports, 1970, 20, 541-543.

36. Templer, D., Russ, C. F., & Franks, C. M. Death
     anxiety: Age, sex and parental resemblance in a
     diverse population. Developmental Psychology,
     1971, 4, 108.

37. Lester, D., & Templer, D. Resemblance of parent-
     child death anxiety as a function of age and sex
     of child. Psychological Reports, 1972, 3, 750.

38. Lowry, R. J. Male-female differences in attitudes
     toward death. Dissertation Abstracts International,
     1966, 27, 1607B-1608B.

39. Kalish, R. A. Some variables in death attitudes.
     Journal of Social Psychology, 1963, 59, 137-145.

40. Hogan, R. A. Adolescent views of death. Adolescence,
     1970, 5(17), 55-56.

41. Lester, D. Attitudes toward death and suicide in a nondisturbed population. Psychological Reports, 1971, 9, 386.

42. Wesch, J. E. Self actualization and the fear of death. Dissertation Abstracts International, 1971, 31, 6270-6271.

43. Lester, D., & Colvin, L. M. Fear of death, alienation, and self actualization. Psychological Reports, 1977, 41, 526.

44. Holinger, P. C. Adolescent suicide-epidemiological-study of recent trends. American Journal of Psychiatry, 1978, 135, 754-756.

45. Toolan, J. M. Suicide in children and adolescents. American Journal of Psychotherapy, 1975, 29, 339-344.

46. Kastenbaum, R. Humans developing: A lifespan perspective. Boston: Allyn & Bacon, 1979.

47. Levinson, D. J., Darrow, C. M., Klein, E. G., Levinson, M. H., & McKee, B. The psychosocial development of men in early adulthood and the mid-life transition. In D. F. Ricks, A. Thomas, & M. Roff (Eds.), Life history research in psychopathology, Vol. 3. Minneapolis: University of Minnesota Press, 1974.

48. Gould, R. L. The phases of adult life: A study in developmental psychology. American Journal of Psychiatry, 1972, 129, 521-531.

49. Vaillant, G. E., & McArthur, C. C. Natural history of male psychological health: The adult life cycle from eighteen to fifty. Seminars in Psychiatry, 1972, 4, 415-427.

50. Katz, S. I. The relationship of the midlife transition to death anxiety and self actualization. Dissertation Abstracts International, 1979, 39, 4035.

51. Berman, A. L., & Hays, J. E. Relation between death anxiety, belief in afterlife and locus of control. Journal of Consulting and Clinical Psychology, 1973, 41, 318.

52. McDonald, G. W. Sex, religion and risk-taking behavior as correlates of death anxiety. Omega, 1976, 7, 35-44.

53. Chasin, B. Neglected variables in the study of
     death attitudes, The Sociological Quarterly, 1971,
     12, 107-113.

54. Bengstrom, U. L., Cuellar, J. B., & Ragan, P. K.
     Stratum contrast and similarities in attitudes
     toward death. Journal of Gerontology, 1977, 32,
     76-78.

55. Gove, W. R. Sex, marital status and mortality,
     American Journal of Sociology, 1973, 79, 45-67.

56. Cole, M. A. Sex and marital status differences in
     death anxiety. Omega, 1978-1979, B9(2), 139-147.

57. Wass, H., Christian, M., Myers, J., & Murphey, M.
     Similarities and dissimilarities in attitudes toward
     death in a population of older persons. Omega,
     1978-1979, 9, 337-363.

58. Zarit, S. H. Aging and mental disorders. New York:
     Free Press, 1980.

59. Templer, D. I. Death anxiety as related to depression
     and health of retired persons. Journal of Geron-
     tology, 1971, 26, 521-523.

60. Kalish, R. A., & Reynolds, D. K. The role of age
     in death attitudes. Death Education, 1977, 1,
     205-230.

61. Moriya, K. Attitudes toward the future: A compara-
     tive study of younger and older samples. Journal
     of Child Development, 1975, 11, 39-44.

62. Rhudick, P. J., & Dibner, A. S. Age, personality
     and health correlates of death concerns in normal
     aged individuals. Journal of Gerontology, 1961,
     16, 44-49.

63. Keily, M. C., & Dudek, S. Z. Attitudes toward
     death in aged persons. The Psychiatric Journal of
     the University of Ottawa, 1977, II(4), 181-184.

64. Christ, P. E. Attitudes toward death among a group
     of acute geriatric psychiatric patients. Journal
     of Gerontology, 1961, 16, 56-59.

65. Wolff, K. The problem of death and dying in the
     geriatric patient. Journal of the American Geriatrics
     Society, 1970, 18, 954-961.

66. Lipman, A., & Marden, P. W. Preparation for death
     in old age. Journal of Gerontology, 1966, 21, 426-
     431.

67. Sanders, J. F., Poole, T. E., & Rivero, W. T.
     Death anxiety among the elderly. Psychological
     Reports, 1980, 46, 53-54.

68. Wass, H., & Sisler, H. H. Death concern and views
     on various aspects of dying among elderly persons.
     In The dying human. Ramat Gan, Israel: Turtledove,
     1979.

69. Jeffers, F. C., Nichols, C. R., & Eisdorfer, C.
     Attitudes of older persons toward death: A prelim-
     inary study. Journal of Gerontology, 1961, 16,
     53-56.

70. Swenson, W. M. Attitudes toward death in an aged
     population. Journal of Gerontology, 1961, 16,
     49-52.

71. Nehrke, M. F., Belluci, G., & Gabriel, S. J. Death
     anxiety, locus of control and life satisfaction in
     the elderly: Toward a definition of ego integrity.
     Omega, 1977-1978, 8, 359-368.

72. Palmore, E. B., & Stone, V. Predictors of longevity:
     A follow-up of the aged in Chapel Hill. The
     Gerontologist, 1973, 13, 88-90.

73. Rowland, K. F. Environmental events predicting
     death for the elderly. Psychological Bulletin,
     1977, 84, 349-372.

74. Moore, R. J., & Newton, J. H. Attitudes of the
     life-threatened hospitalized elderly. Essence,
     1977, 3, 129-138.

75. Kleemeier, R. W. Intellectual changes in the
     senium, or death and the IQ. Presidential address,
     Division 20, American Psychological Association,
     New York, September 1961.

76. Jarvik, L. F., & Falek, A. Intellectual stability
     and survival in the aged. Journal of Gerontology,
     1963, 18, 173-176.

77. Lieberman, M. A. Psychological correlates of
     impending death. Journal of Gerontology, 1965, 20,
     181-190.

78. Bascue, L. O., & Lawrence, R. E. A study of sub-
     jective time and death anxiety in the elderly.
     Omega, 1977, 8, 81-90.

79. Riegel, K. F. The predictors of death and longevity
     in longitudinal research. In E. Palmore & F. C.

Jeffers (Eds.), Prediction of life span. Lexington, Mass.: Heath, 1971.

80. Botwinick, J., West, R., & Storandt, M. Predicting death from behavioral test performance. Journal of Gerontology, 1978, 33, 755-762.

81. Lieberman, M. A., & Coplen, A. S. Distance from death as a variable in the study of aging. Developmental Psychology, 1969, 2, 71-84.

82. Schulz, C. M. Death anxiety and the structuring of a death concerns cognitive domain, Essence, 1977, 3, 171-188.

MURDER, SUICIDE, AND THE SEXES

One murder made a villain,
Millions a hero.--Princes were privileged
to kill, and numbers sanctified the crime.
Ah! Why will kings forget that they are men,
And men that they are brethren?

Bishop Porteus
Death

Suicide.....is about life, being in fact
the sincerest form of criticism life gets.

Wilfrid Sheed
The Good Word

INTRODUCTION

In the past two decades, the United States has repeatedly
been characterized as a "sick society." Generally these
characterizations become more widespread after an
assassination or attempted assassination. The deaths
of John F. Kennedy, Malcolm X, Martin Luther King,
Robert Kennedy, and the more recent attempt on the life
of Ronald Reagan, have focused attention on the increase
in violence within American life. Henry and Short in
1954 noted that 8,000 people were murdered and 17,000
took their own lives each year in the United States (1).
In 1983, the comparable figures were estimated to be
20,781 deaths from homicide and 27,510 deaths from suicide
(2). Taken together, homicide and suicide deaths account
for one death out of approximately every forty (3).

Although there are many differences between people who
commit murder and those who commit suicide, the two

71

causes of death have one thing in common. They do not
have to happen. While individuals generally cannot
decide not to die of cancer or heart disease, theoreti-
cally they can make a rational decision not to take a
life, either their own or someone else's. They also can
often decide to avoid circumstances that would make them
potential homicide or suicide victims. Available
statistics seem to support the hypothesis that females
are more successful in making these decisions.

The purpose of this chapter is to examine in depth the sex
differential in homicide and suicide as well as to suggest
multiple factors that might be implicated in the sex differential in violent death. A large body of research is
beginning to be generated on the topic of murder. An even
larger one exists on the topic of suicide. It is beyond
the scope of this chapter to review all the available data
on these two topics. We will attempt to examine only
certain classical and recent studies that shed light on the
sex differential in homicide and suicide. Among the questions to be addressed in this chapter are the following:
Why are females less likely to commit murder, suicide, and
to become murder victims than are males? Are there certain
types of violent crimes that women commit more frequently
than do men? What are the characteristics of women who
commit murder, and how are they different from those of men
who commit murder? How do males and females differ in
suicide and suicide attempts? What possible explanations
can be proposed for the sex differential in murder and
suicide? Are statistics on homicide and suicide changing
as women's roles change under the influence of the new
feminism?

WOMEN, MEN, AND MURDER

Let us begin by looking at the differential worlds of
male and female killers. Males live in a more violent
world than do females. The stereotype of the male as
the aggressive, violent criminal is overwhelmingly
accepted in our culture. To test this, ask any group
of people to close their eyes and visualize a criminal.
Ask them to "zoom in" on the criminal's face just as a
TV camera zooms in on its target. Instruct them to
visualize clearly the hair, facial features, clothing
and shoes. Give them a few seconds to sharpen their
visualizations. The shared visualizations, if they
follow the general patterns, will be overwhelmingly,
if not unanimously, male. Furthermore, they will often
reflect nonwhite racial and low socioeconomic status as
well as relatively young age. What this exercise
illustrates is that most people have absorbed enough
information about crime and criminals to reflect fairly
accurately the existing situation in their stereotypes.
Males are more often the acting-out aggressive criminals.

They are also more often the victims of homicide. This is true geographically as well as historically.

One source contrasts figures for seven nonliterate African societies with those for England and Wales and the United States. The seven African countries reported over 90 percent male homicide offenders, while for England and Wales over a 49-year period, 68 percent of the offenders were male (4). In the United States, male rates were estimated at three to nine times as high as female rates. A review of six studies reported percentages of male homicide at between 74 percent and 90 percent, depending upon place and period of time (4).

Another widely quoted source conducted a study of 404 homicide defendants and their 432 victims (5). Males were found to be four times more likely to be arrested for homicide and two times as likely to be victims of homicide as were females. Table 4.1 shows homicide rates per 100,000 population for 27 different countries across a recent four-year period. It can be noted that all countries with the exception of Denmark show a higher homicide rate for males than for females. It should also be noted that in the three countries that have the highest homicide rates (Puerto Rico, Northern Ireland, and the United States), the discrepancy between male and female homicide deaths increases.

Wolfgang cites two authors who address the question of differential rates in homicide (6). One of them, Verkko, believes that there is a rule governing sex differential in homicide. Basing his claim on a historical study of data from Sweden, Verkko stated that if homicide rates are high in a country, women's participation as killers will be proportionately low, but where there is a low frequency of killings, women's proportional participation will be perceptibly higher. Verkko further believed that the "distribution by sexes of victims of crimes against life in any country is always dependent on the frequency level of the crime committed" (6, p. 61). The second author, Brearly, has also called attention to the same phenomenon by noting that as homicide rates go up in a country, the proportion of females killed goes down. Brearly contrasted the homicide rates in England and the United States by pointing out that the relatively low English rate includes two out of three women as victims while the relatively high U.S. rate includes one woman victim to approximately four men victims. Lester (7) tested this hypothesis by examining the homicide rates in 33 countries that were members of the United Nations. He found that the 16 countries that had the highest homicide rates did have a lower proportion of female victims than did the 16 countries with the lowest homicide rates. What all this seems to mean is that, compared to males, females'

TABLE 4.1 Homicide and Suicide Rates, by Selected
Countries: 1975 to 1978 (Homicide rates per 100,000
population of all ages, suicide rates per 100,000 population 15 years old and over)

	Homicides							
	Male				Female			
Country	1975	1976	1977	1978	1975	1976	1977	1978
U.S.	16.0	14.5	14.6	(NA)	4.4	4.0	4.2	(NA)
Australia	2.1	2.5	2.4	(NA)	1.2	1.6	1.5	(NA)
Austria	2.1	1.4	1.4	1.6	1.3	1.1	1.3	1.2
Belgium	1.3	1.0	(NA)	(NA)	.5	.9	(NA)	(NA)
Canada	3.6	(NA)	3.5	(NA)	1.8	(NA)	1.7	(NA)
Denmark	.5	.6	.7	.6	.7	.8	.7	.4
Finland	5.8	(NA)	(NA)	(NA)	1.6	(NA)	(NA)	(NA)
France	1.3	1.2	(NA)	(NA)	.7	.6	(NA)	(NA)
Germany (Fed. Rep)	1.4	1.4	1.4	1.4	1.0	1.1	1.0	1.1
Greece	1.2	.9	.8	1.1	.4	.4	.5	.3
Ireland	1.3	(NA)	(NA)	(NA)	.6	(NA)	(NA)	(NA)
Israel[1]	1.7	1.9	2.2	2.2	1.8	.9	.7	1.0
Japan	1.6	1.5	1.5	1.3	1.0	1.0	1.0	.9
Nether-lands	1.0	1.0	1.2	1.0	.4	.6	.6	.6
Norway	.9	.9	1.2	1.0	.5	.6	.4	.5
Philip-pines	2.5	(NA)	(NA)	(NA)	.3	(NA)	(NA)	(NA)
Poland	1.3	1.7	1.7	1.7	.8	.8	.9	.9
Portugal	3.4	(NA)	(NA)	(NA)	.5	(NA)	(NA)	(NA)
Puerto Rico	29.3	(NA)	(NA)	(NA)	3.5	(NA)	(NA)	(NA)
Spain	1.0	(NA)	(NA)	(NA)	.3	(NA)	(NA)	(NA)
Sweden	1.5	1.5	1.6	1.4	.8	1.0	.8	.6
Switzer-land	1.0	.9	1.0	.8	.9	.9	.7	.7
U.K. England[2]	1.2	1.2	1.0	(NA)	.8	1.0	.8	(NA)
Northern Ireland	20.8	24.2	25.0	(NA)	2.3	3.3	3.9	(NA)
Scotland	2.1	2.9	2.8	1.9	.9	1.1	1.1	1.1

Footnotes on following page.

TABLE 4.1 Homicide and Suicide Rates, by Selected
Countries: 1975 to 1978 (Homicide rates per 100,000
population of all ages, suicide rates per 100,000 population 15 years old and over) (Cont'd)

	Suicides							
	Male				Female			
Country	1975	1976	1977	1978	1975	1976	1977	1978
U.S.	25.5	24.9	26.5	(NA)	8.9	8.6	8.8	(NA)
Australia	20.9	21.7	21.9	(NA)	9.5	7.9	8.4	(NA)
Austria	47.4	43.6	45.3	47.2	17.6	17.0	18.8	17.8
Belgium	27.4	28.4	(NA)	(NA)	14,6	14.4	(NA)	(NA)
Canada	24.5	(NA)	28.3	(NA)	9.2	(NA)	9.6	(NA)
Denmark	38.8	39.2	39.9	36.0	23.6	22.6	22.6	23.7
Finland	52.6	(NA)	(NA)	(NA)	13.2	(NA)	(NA)	(NA)
France	30.0	29.8	(NA)	(NA)	11.5	11.5	(NA)	(NA)
Germany (Fed. Rep)	35.8	37.2	38.3	37.7	18.2	18.5	19.5	18.4
Greece	4.6	5.0	6.2	5.5	2.6	2.3	2.6	2.0
Ireland	9.7	(NA)	(NA)	(NA)	4.1	(NA)	(NA)	(NA)
Israel[1]	13.8	14.9	12.5	9.9	10.0	8.8	7.0	6.9
Japan	28.5	28.2	29.3	29.2	18.9	18.3	17.9	17.3
Netherlands	14.5	15.8	15.2	14.5	9.3	9.3	9.0	10.7
Norway	18.6	21.1	22.2	22.7	7.2	7.3	7.6	7.7
Philippines	1.7	(NA)	(NA)	(NA)	1.4	(NA)	(NA)	(NA)
Poland	25.6	27.1	27.8	30.0	4.8	5.2	5.2	5.4
Portugal	18.9	(NA)	(NA)	(NA)	5.5	(NA)	(NA)	(NA)
Puerto Rico	20.7	(NA)	(NA)	(NA)	3.6	(NA)	(NA)	(NA)
Spain	8.3	(NA)	(NA)	(NA)	2.7	(NA)	(NA)	(NA)
Sweden	35.2	33.6	35.6	33.1	13.8	14.1	13.9	14.7
Switzerland	42.3	41.4	43.5	43.5	16.4	15.9	17.9	17.8
U.K. England[2]	12.9	12.8	12.9	(NA)	7.6	7.5	7.9	(NA)
Northern Ireland	6.8	7.9	7.1	(NA)	3.6	4.6	5.6	(NA)
Scotland	12.1	13.3	13.1	14.5	9.6	8.7	8.4	7.8

NA Not available
[1]Jewish population
[2]Includes Wales
Source: World Health Organization, Geneva, Switzerland, unpublished
data.

TABLE 4.2 Homicide and Suicide Victims, by Race and Sex: 1950 to 1978 (Rates per 100,000 resident population in specified group. Beginning 1970, excludes deaths to nonresidents of U.S.)

| | | Homicide Victims | | | | | Suicide Victims | | | | |
| | | | White | | Black/Other | | | White | | Black/Other | |
Year	Total	Male	Female	Male	Female	Total	Male	Female	Male	Female
						Number				
1950	7,942	2,586	952	3,503	901	17,145	12,755	3,713	542	135
1955	7,418	2,439	922	3,191	866	16,760	12,430	3,662	531	137
1960	8,464	2,832	1,154	3,437	1,041	19,041	13,825	4,296	714	206
1965	10,712	3,660	1,379	4,488	1,185	21,507	14,424	5,718	866	299
1968	14,686	5,106	1,700	6,417	1,463	21,372	14,520	5,692	859	301
1969	15,477	5,215	1,801	6,951	1,510	22,364	14,886	6,152	971	355
1970	16,848	5,865	1,938	7,413	1,632	23,480	15,591	6,468	1,038	383
1971	18,737	6,455	2,106	8,357	1,869	24,092	15,802	6,775	1,058	457
1972 1	19,638	6,820	2,156	8,822	1,840	25,004	16,476	6,788	1,292	448
1973	20,465	7,411	2,575	8,429	2,050	25,118	16,823	6,589	1,285	421
1974	21,465	7,992	2,656	8,755	2,062	25,683	17,263	6,660	1,332	428
1975	21,310	8,222	2,751	8,331	2,063	27,063	18,206	6,967	1,416	474
1976	19,544	7,568	2,547	7,574	1,865	26,832	17,996	6,858	1,497	481
1977	19,968	7,951	2,787	7,404	1,826	28,681	19,531	7,048	1,578	524
1978	20,432	8,429	2,771	7,409	1,823	22,294	18,619	6,631	1,569	475

Footnote on following page

TABLE 4.2 Homicide and Suicide Victims, by Race and Sex: 1950 to 1978 (Rates per 100,000 resident population in specified group. Beginning 1970, excludes deaths to nonresidents of U.S.) (Cont'd)

Year	Homicide Victims Total	Homicide White Male	Homicide White Female	Homicide Black/Other Male	Homicide Black/Other Female	Suicide Victims Total (Rate[2])	Suicide White Male	Suicide White Female	Suicide Black/Other Male	Suicide Black/Other Female
1950	5.2	3.8	1.4	44.2	10.9	11.3	19.0	5.5	6.8	1.6
1955	4.5	3.4	1.2	36.0	9.3	10.2	17.1	4.9	6.0	1.5
1960	4.7	3.6	1.4	34.3	9.8	10.6	17.6	5.3	7.1	1.9
1965	5.5	4.4	1.6	40.4	10.0	11.1	17.5	6.6	7.8	2.5
1968	7.4	6.0	1.9	55.1	11.6	10.7	17.0	6.4	7.4	2.4
1969	7.7	6.1	2.0	58.7	11.7	11.1	17.3	6.8	8.2	2.7
1970	8.3	6.7	2.1	61.4	12.4	11.5	17.9	7.1	8.6	2.9
1971	9.1	7.3	2.3	67.7	13.9	11.7	17.9	7.3	8.6	3.4
1972[1]	9.4	7.7	2.3	70.1	13.4	12.0	18.5	7.3	10.3	3.3
1973	9.8	8.3	2.8	65.8	14.6	12.0	18.8	7.0	10.0	3.0
1974	10.2	8.9	2.8	67.1	14.5	12.1	19.2	7.1	10.2	3.0
1975	10.0	9.1	2.9	62.6	13.8	12.7	20.1	7.4	10.6	3.3
1976	9.1	8.3	2.7	55.8	12.5	12.5	19.8	7.2	11.0	3.2
1977	9.2	8.7	2.9	53.6	12.0	13.3	21.4	7.3	11.4	3.5
1978	9.4	9.2	2.9	52.6	11.8	12.5	20.2	6.9	11.1	3.1

[1]Based on a 50 percent sample of deaths.
[2]Rate based on enumerated population figures of April 1 for 1950, 1960, and 1970; July estimates for other years.
Source: U.S. National Center for Health Statistics, Vital Statistics of the Unites States, annual.

participation in homicide both as victim and as killer has
been more constant: less susceptible to fluctuation.
Whether it will continue to be so as gender roles change
is a question we will consider later in the chapter.

Our recent history in the United States indicates that
homicide is on the increase, therefore providing some
support for those critics who maintain we are a sick
society. Table 4.2 shows homicide and suicide rates for
males and females in the United States by race from 1950-
1978. Two important observations regarding homicide can
be made from this table.

First, we would be remiss if we did not point out that
blacks and other nonwhites have a much greater frequency
of death by murder than do whites. Indeed, the table
shows that the differential between the races is greater
than that between the sexes. For nonwhite males, homicide
is the fourth leading cause of death. It is the leading
cause of death for black men and women between the ages of
25 and 34, accounting for approximately one-third of all
male deaths and one-sixth of all female deaths. Eliminating
homicide as a cause of death among black males would add
approximately a year-and-a-half to their life expectancy
at birth while it would add only .38 of a year for black
females, .21 of a year for white males, and .08 of a year
for white females (2). Second, male rates of homicide
exceed female rates across the 28-year-period by at least
a 3 to 1 ratio.

In addition to gender and racial factors, age and education play a role in homicide figures, but the role is
slightly different for men and women. Table 4.3 shows
the percent of persons arrested for murder and nonnegligent
manslaughter by age for the year 1981. Males made up
87.3 percent of the persons arrested for murder and nonnegligent manslaughter during that year. It can be seen
in the table that 79.9 percent of all people arrested
for killings were between the ages of 18 and 44. Women

TABLE 4.3   Percent of Persons Arrested for Murder and
Nonnegligent Manslaughter by Age (years)--1981

Under 15	Under 18	18-24	25-44	45-54	55-64	65+
1.0	9.1	34.1	45.8	6.4	3.1	1.5

Source: Statistical abstract of the United States, 103d Edition,
p. 182. Washington, D.C.: U.S. Bureau of the Census, 1980.

TABLE 4.4   Percent of Defendants Engaged in Selected
Occupations

Occupation	Male	Female
Major professionals	.6	-
Managers, proprietors, and lesser professionals	.3	2.4
Administrative personnel, small business owners, and minor professionals	2.6	1.2
Clerical and kindred workers	4.5	5.9
Skilled laborors	14.1	8.2
Semiskilled laborors	15.3	10.6
Unskilled laborors	31.6	45.9

Source: Swigert, V., & Farrell, R.   Murder, inequality, and the
law.   Mass.: D.C. Heath, 1976.

tend to become murderers at a slightly older age than do
men (8).   Women arrested for murder also tend to be
slightly more educated than their counterparts.   One
study showed that 28 percent of female defendants had
at least completed high school compared to 24.6 percent
of the male defendants (5).

The same study reported sex differences in occupations
among defendants, as shown in Table 4.4.   It is clear
from the table that the incidence of arrest for murder
of both males and females increases as socioeconomic
status decreases, thus introducing yet another factor
into the complex prediction equation of who kills.
Females, it should be noted, are overrepresented compared
to males in the category of unskilled laborers.

Swigert and Farrell also attempted to classify defendants
as to the motives involved in their homicides (see Table
4.5).   Once again it is clear that sex differences exist
with regard to motives for killing, with females far
outnumbering males in the killing of family members as a
part of a family fight.   Women, at least according to
this study, rarely kill because they are involved in an
argument with strangers or because of accidental circumstances.   They are also less likely than males to kill
as a result of being involved in another criminal offense.
They are almost equally as likely as are males to kill
because of an argument with friends or because of a
psychotic reaction.   The authors of this study stress
the point that the great majority of killings, done by
both males and females, occur among people who know each

TABLE 4.5   Motives of Defendants in Homicide Cases by Sex Expressed in Percent

Motive	Male	Female
Family fight	29.9	60.7
Argument with friends	29.9	28.1
Neighbors or acquaintances		
Transfer of intent (result of criminal offenses and robbery)	21.8	6.7
Psychotic reaction	3.3	2.2
Arguments with strangers	10.3	1.1
Alleged accident	4.8	1.1

Source: Swigert, V., & Farrell, R., Murder, inequality and the law. Mass.: D.E. Heath, 1976.

other rather than with strangers. They maintain that 60 percent of male-committed murders and almost 90 percent of female-committed murders have victims who are family, friends, or acquaintances.

Other studies cite different percentages. For example, Wolfgang (6) found in his Philadelphia samples that 52 percent of female killers were likely to have family members as victims compared to 16 percent of males who killed. Palmer, citing statistics in England and Wales, found that 81 percent of females killed family members compared to 37 percent of males (4).

Some observers of the criminal scene suggest that women are more treacherous than men because, when they do kill, they more often kill those who are close to them. However, an alternative explanation is that of lack of opportunity. Traditionally, women have been more circumscribed in their relationships than men have been. They have also moved in smaller, more limited life spaces and thus have not been able to move out into a world of strangers to find their victims. Simply stated, in order to kill someone, you must be physically close to them. Women, at least in the past, have been physically close only to family and a limited number of friends. Indirect support for the lack of opportunity hypothesis may be found in the fact that females who kill are less likely to have an arrest record than are males (6). Engaging in criminal activities requires a greater amount of freedom than many traditionally reared women have enjoyed.

The nature of murders seems to vary by sexes also. For example, one study that examined killings in California between 1960 and 1970 reported that male victims were killed more frequently by firearms or knives; female victims were killed more frequently by beatings and kickings (9). While victims of both sexes tend to be killed more frequently in their homes than in any other place, female murderers tend to kill most frequently in the kitchen or bedroom while males kill most frequently on the highway, followed by the bedroom (6). The degree of violence surrounding killings also differs by sex. One study showed that only 33 percent of female homicides showed a high degree of violence compared to almost 54.5 percent of male homicides. Violence in this case refers to the number of physical acts committed against the victim before, during, or after the actual killing. It should be noted that among women victims, over 62 percent showed high violence accompanying their deaths compared to 46 percent of male victims (6).

More husbands than wives seem to be involved in "victim-precipitated killings," i.e., killings that occur as a result of actions (sometimes repeated over a long period of time) of the victim (6). The classic example of victim-precipitated murder is that of the husband who continuously batters his wife. One day he may come home drunk and/or tired. She may be afraid that he will beat her when he recovers or she may just have been beaten. In either case, she waits for him to fall asleep and then kills him. However, although there is a sex differential in victim-precipitated murder, it should be remembered that women are represented in this category. A good example of a female precipitating her own murder is recounted in Houts' book, They Asked For Death (10). Houts reviews the case of a wife who nagged her husband for 41 years, systematically attacking his self-esteem. Finally, she goaded him into killing her with these words: "Go ahead and try it--I don't think you've got the guts. I know you haven't got the guts. You'd bollix that up the way you've done everything else in life if you tried. You know better than to try. I'll tell you exactly what I think of you any time I want to and for as long as I want to" (p. 126). Her husband strangled her to death.

Another sex difference in murder appears in the killing of children, a type of murder that is more frequent than generally supposed. One study showed that one out of every 22 murder victims in the year 1966 was a child killed by his/her own parent and that murders of children over 24 hours old were committed twice as frequently by mothers as by fathers while neonaticides (killings of newborns) were committed almost totally by women (11). The author of the study, Resnick, cited five motives that seemed to characterize the female murderers of their children. The first he called altruistic filicide, or the killing of a child out of love and pity in order to

prevent real or imagined later suffering. Second,
mothers killed children because they were unwanted.
These children might have been illegitimate or just one
too many in an already overburdened home. The third
motive was described as getting even with a spouse by
killing his favorite child. Fourth, there are those
cases when punishment accelerates into murder. Resnick
characterized these as instances of accidental filicide.
The final category was called acutely psychotic filicide
and refers to those child killings that occur as a
result of insane actions on the part of the parent.
Resnick found that the murdering mothers were twice as
likely to be diagnosed as depressed as were the murdering fathers. In addition, men who killed their children
were more likely to be judged nonpsychotic than were
women who committed filicide (11, 12). This finding was
supported in a study by Myers, who found the majority
of filicidal mothers were judged to be psychotic while
the fathers were judged to be sane and sentenced to
prison. Women who kill infants under 24 hours old are
seen less as psychotic and more as dependent and immature
(13).

Women are also more likely to murder elderly dependents
and handicapped persons than are men. This is probably
due to two circumstances. First, females are more often
the responsible parties for such people. If a male
living with a handicapped person or the elderly gets
tired of being around them, he can traditionally leave
the house; stay away an evening or a week and know that
they will be cared for by the woman of the house. But
what does the woman of the house do when she is fed up?
Traditionally she "keeps on keeping on." The only alternative many times is to break down, becoming sick or
suicidal or perhaps killing the elderly parent or handicapped sibling. These same circumstances probably also
feed into higher maternal murders. The second circumstance
is simply that there is a good chance of success for the
woman in completing the killing. The potential victims
are in some way vulnerable and, in contrast to her
strength relative to men, the female killer can physically
overpower these people. One study that examined the
victims of such murderers, omitting instances of infanti-
cide, found that 21 percent were children; 15 percent
were seriously ill or crippled; 9 percent were older than
70 or mentally ill; and 16 percent were drunk at the time
of the slaying (14). In sum, this study found that 61
percent of the 125 female offenders' victims could defend
themselves only to a limited extent. The author of the
study contrasted the motives of the female murderers in
the study to those generally assigned to male murderers
with the following description: "...most women killers
were not motivated by material interest or by sudden
impulse but rather by long lasting emotional conflict
situations. The commission of the crime was the overt

manifestation of their latest aggression, which had often been repressed for a long time" (14, p. 401).

Additional information concerning the female murderer is available from several sources. Totman (15) reported figures that she found in two states of the United States and which were almost duplicates of those found in a Hungarian study. She found that 40 percent of female murderers' victims were husbands, common-law husbands or lovers, while 21 percent were children and 39 percent were other relatives, acquaintances, or strangers. Eysenck and Eysenck found that female murderers were regarded as more disturbed than were male murderers as well as more difficult to handle (16). It is difficult to know whether female murderers are regarded this way because they have so abruptly departed from the stereo- typic traits of nurturance and passivity that are generally expected of women, or whether these women are truly more disturbed than men and therefore have been able to de- part from societal expectations. However, the Eysencks are among those who believe that female killers are really more disturbed than are male killers.

In an attempt to classify the motivations of female killers in more depth, a group of investigators examined 11 female killers and their crimes (17). While 11 cases are not enough to formulate a universal theory, they are suggestive of categories of female killing and thus may prove useful in future studies. The six categories identified are described below:

1. Masochistic--These female killers were stable people who had good reputations. They were often religious and often employed outside the home. However, they were married to abusive, unstable males and often killed them while being beaten. This type of woman showed sorrow, remorse, and depression after the killing.

2. Overtly hostile--These women were aggressive, impul- sive, and emotionally unstable. They showed little guilt or depression after the killing but did report some sense of loss.

3. Covertly hostile--This group was able to express hostility only when in safe situations. They fre- quently killed their children. They often were poor homemakers and mothers before the killing, and showed little remorse or sense of loss after the fact.

4. Psychotic--These women were chronically disturbed and showed poor interpersonal relationships. They often did not recall the crime, showed flat affect, and no remorse.

5. Amoral--This type of woman killed deliberately for economic gain or to remove someone from the scene who was blocking her in a heterosexual relationship. Of all the categories, this is the one in which the woman may have a record of past antisocial or criminal behavior. Although the woman in this category is often intelligent, she tends to treat people as objects.

6. Inadequate--Female killers in this category showed little coping ability. They were often very dependent on a dominant husband or friend and sometimes murdered on the orders of this dominant person. They tended to show confusion as well as flattened affect and/or below average intelligence.

When we move from considering women as murderers to women as victims, we must become aware that a large number of crimes entered into the statistics books as homicides are really femicides; that is, the victims are women rather than men. Russell and Van de Ven point out that men's greater physical strength and generally greater readiness to use violence affects all relationships between women and men (18). There are sexual politics involved in murder, as many killings occur as a result of a battle for control and superiority in relationships. It has been estimated that one out of every 10 female murder victims in the United States is killed during rape or other sexual offenses (18), perhaps the ultimate situation of male-female conflict. Older women, who have had a lifetime to acquire material goods, are doubly vulnerable; first, because of their relative female weakness and second, because of the weakness imposed by age. Schafer (19) has pointed out that many crimes are actually precipitated unconsciously by the weakness of the victim. If this is true then aged, sick, or handicapped women are natural victims. In some countries, female victims have actually outnumbered males. For example, Schafer reports that in England and Wales female homicide victims outnumber males 3 to 2 while in the United States, at the same time, only 43 percent of homicide victims are female. More recent victimization figures for the two areas are cited by Palmer (20). He found that the sex of homicide victims in England and Wales in the mid-1970s was almost evenly divided, while in the United States the female victimization rate was one-quarter that of the male rate. Females under one year of age in both countries had higher victimization rates than males and higher rates than the rates for females of all ages combined.

One study attempted to analyze the role that drug usage might play in increasing women's likelihood of becoming homicide victims (21). Zahn compared all homicide victims who were drug users in Philadelphia during the year 1969 to a random sample of homicide victims who were not drug users. Demographically, no differences were found between the two groups on race, religion, or marital status, although the drug-using victims were more likely to be employed or in school than were the victims not on drugs. Drug users were also younger than nondrug users and were more likely to have a criminal record. While both groups of women were most likely to be killed by husbands or lovers, the drug-using women were more frequently killed by storekeepers, private police, and family members other than a spouse. The importance of this study is that it focuses on a group of women victims who are nontraditional and is able to show differences between them and more traditional women victims. Thus the study suggests that as women become involved in different types of life-styles, the circumstances surrounding their violent deaths will also change.

Summary

We have seen that women are less prone to commit murder and to become victims of murder than are men. Both sexes tend to kill family, friends, and acquaintances more often than strangers, although this is even more true of women than of men. Females also kill newborns, children, and aged, weak, and helpless persons more often than do males. Males and females tend to choose different weapons and different places for killing, with females killing most often with knives in the kitchen; males most often beat or shoot their victims in the bedroom or on the highway. Female murderers tend to be older than males, slightly better educated, and tend more often than males to be on welfare. The incidence of killing among both males and females goes up as socio-economic and occupational status go down. Males tend to exhibit higher levels of violence in their killings. Women, because of their physical constitution, seem to be natural victims. There is a higher proportion of women victims of murder than female murderers. Many of these murders occur in conjunction with rape or to older women who seem comparatively wealthy. Women drug users, as members of a nontraditional subculture, often experience different circumstances in dying than do their more traditional sisters. Murders of males by female murderers as compared to murders of females by males can more often be characterized as victim-precipitated crimes. The sex differences in the area of homicide are many and varied and point up the complexity involved in attempting to understand the differential worlds of men and women.

WOMEN, MEN, AND SUICIDE

Let us begin this section by establishing the fact that
males commit suicide at a higher rate than do females.
Table 4.2 (pages 76, 77) also presents suicide rates in
the United States by sex and race for the years 1950 to
1978. The following information can be gleaned from
the table. First, total male suicide rates have consistently been approximately three times that of
females. Second, suicide rates for both categories--
black and other minority as well as white males--have
increased across the eight-year period, while those for
black females have increased only slightly and those
for white females have actually decreased slightly. The
increases for white males occurred in the adolescent
and young adult age ranges while those for black males
included those two age ranges but also showed an increase
in suicide rates during the middle years, ages 35-44.
White females between the ages of 15 and 24 showed a
slight increase in suicide, but it was more than balanced
by decreases in other age ranges. Black and other
minority females show a different pattern, with suicide
actually diminishing slightly during adolescence and
young adulthood but increasing slightly between the ages
of 35 and 64 before decreasing again.

In contrast to successful suicides, however, the rate
of attempted suicide is higher for women than for men.
In fact, the statistics in the two categories are almost
mirror images of each other. The number of successful
suicides by males compared to the number of suicide
attempts by females in four studies reviewed by Gove
will emphasize this point (22). The figures and their
appropriate studies of origin are indicated in Table 4.6.

Another study reviewed suicide attempts in different
countries as reported in studies published since 1971 (23).

TABLE 4.6 Percentage of Suicides Completed by Males
Compared to Percentages of Female Attempts

Researcher	Year	Male success (%)	Female attempts (%)
Shneidman and Farberau	1961	70.3	68.8
Pokorny	1965	73.1	72.0
Edwards and Whitlock	1968	53	71
McCaslin	Unpublished data	78.4	72.9

The authors found 14 studies which included figures for both male and female suicide attempts. All but one of these studies showed a preponderance of female attempters. This is particularly impressive in light of the fact that almost all of these studies were based on hospital statistics, and only the most serious suicide attempts reach the hospital. Males tend to use more aggressive methods in their suicide attempts and are therefore more likely to be overrepresented in the hospital statistics than are female attempters, who use less violent means.

Males are more likely to try suicide by shooting, stabbing, or hanging, while females most often attempt it by drug ingestion. Marks (24) found that both women and men tended to reflect sex role stereotypes in considering different methods of suicide. For example, women stated that they would prefer easily available, nonmessy and painless methods, while men wanted effective, efficient methods. Some people have speculated that drug ingestion attempts represent less serious suicide attempts--that they are more often cries for help (25). Others feel the sex difference in type of attempts can be directly traced to socialization toward independence and success for males as contrasted with dependence, passivity, preoccupation with physical appearance, and external orientation for females (26). Marks (24) is one researcher who concluded that the specific methods chosen by each sex do not indicate the seriousness of the suicide attempt. He felt that both men and women attempting suicide were equally likely to be serious. He pointed out, however, that the "feminine" methods of attempting suicide (e.g., drugs or poison) were more likely to leave time for possible rescue attempts or for changing one's mind than were the more violent "masculine" methods. The type of method chosen, however, can only partially explain the sex difference in successful suicide, as males are more successful in every method of committing suicide than are females.

Suicide rates seem to vary across occupational groups. Several studies have reported that women in the predominantly male professions have a higher rate of suicide than women in more traditional female occupations. Newman, Whittemore, and Newman, for example, found that suicide rate is related to female labor force participation (27). In considering suicide rates, they suggested that "entry of women into the labor force has relevance, particularly for the woman who takes on an additional role as 'breadwinner' in addition to being a wife and/or mother. The additional position provides opportunity for role conflict, particularly among higher status women, where demands on their time as a part of their job may be high" (p. 226). Diamond (28) found that among a group of women professionals, the attempters of

suicide generally reported a significantly greater number
of role conflicts. More specifically, the attempters
reported more conflict between their roles as a woman
and as a professional than did those professional women
who had not attempted suicide. Pitts, Schuler, Rich,
and Pitts (29) examined all American Medical Association
records of deaths of female physicians for the five-year
period between 1967 and 1972. They found that the rate
of suicide among female doctors was 40.7 per 100,000 compared to a male rate of 38.1 per 100,000. That rate
of suicide is four times as high as that of other American
white women over age 24 and twice as high as that for
divorced women over age 70, which is the group of women
in the general population at highest risk. Female
psychologists have also been found to have a suicide
rate three times that of women in the general population
(30). These studies taken together offer some support
for the suggestion that the role conflict of women
engaged in predominantly male occupations is severe
enough to increase the risk of suicide.

A study with somewhat different findings, however, was
reported by Taylor (31). He examined the effects of
work roles and labor force participation on female rates
of suicide from 1968-1972. He found that the employed
of both sexes have higher than average rates of suicide.
In addition, he found higher rates of suicide for people
of both sexes who were engaged in low status occupations.
He suggested that if male and female suicide rates were
standardized according to occupation, males and females
employed in the same occupational categories would be
equally represented in the suicide statistics. Clearly
he feels that higher male suicide rates are to a great
extent based on the fact that many more males than
females are employed in occupations having low status.

Marital status is a third factor which has been investi-
gated in suicide studies. Gove (22) found that there
was "a greater disparity between being married and being
single [widowed, divorced] for men than for women" (p.
204). He concluded that marriage has more advantages
for males than for females while singlehood, including
divorced and widowed categories, is worse for men than
for women in terms of suicidal outcomes. (As an aside,
this research supports later research that shows that
marriage is significantly better for males than for
females in terms of general mental health and life
satisfaction, e.g., 32, 33.) Both divorce and widowhood
seem to increase suicidal tendencies. Jacobson and
Portuges (34) found that 39 percent of 238 subjects who
were considering divorce or were recently widowed were
suicidal, a percentage much higher than would be
expected by chance. They did not, however, report sex
differences among their divorcing population. Another
study, conducted by Herman (35), examined divorce as a

crisis among 200 women. Herman maintained that divorce
leads to depression and feelings of hopelessness among
women which are "compounded by inadequate role development which prevents their [women's] subsequent integration
into the economic, legal, political and social structures
of society" (p. 107). Wenz (36) examined the suicide
rate among widowed and divorced people in one subpopula-
tion of Flint, Michigan, and found it to be nine times
greater than in the rest of the city. He found that
the female suicide rate was 1.4 times greater than that
of the males in the population. He, like Herman, suggested that social ties were important in guarding
against suicide. Males, when compared to homebound
females, may have more opportunities to find social outlets, especially if the female has been socialized toward
passivity and dependence. The importance of social ties
will be explored further in the next chapter in conjunction with grief resolution.

Summary

Males in the United States commit suicide approximately
three times as often as do females. Females attempt
suicide approximately three times as often as do males.
Age distribution patterns for male and female suicides
are different. Female suicide rates are highest in the
middle years and lowest in the youngest and oldest groups,
while male suicide rates increase with increasing age.
Suicide rates also differ by race, with whites of both
sexes having higher rates of suicide than blacks and
other minority groups. Males tend to use more violent
means of committing suicide. However, they outnumber
females in every type of successful suicide. Research
as to the role occupations play in suicide is contradictory. However, it does seem clear that female physicians
and psychologists have higher rates of suicide than do
other women in the population. The married of both sexes
have a lower rate of suicide than do single, widowed,
or divorced people. However, married males seem to be
particularly advantaged. Divorce and widowhood seem to
increase suicidal risk, particularly for those without
extensive social ties.

SPECULATIONS CONCERNING SEX DIFFERENCES IN MURDER AND
SUICIDE

When thinking people are confronted with the evidence
that shows that males are murderers, victims of murder,
and successful victims of suicide more often than are
females, they generally begin to look for causes for
such statistics. To date, causes are far from clear.
However, there are some intriguing suggestions as to
possible variables which, when taken together, may begin

to help us understand the sex differential in murder and
suicide. Since the following sections are based on preliminary data--generally observational or case study
material, occasionally including correlational studies--
we have tried to stress the tentative nature of the
following material in the heading of the remainder of
the chapter, "Speculations Concerning Sex Differences
in Murder and Suicide." In reviewing earlier studies
in this chapter, we have suggested a few leads concerning
underlying causes when the researchers made such a discussion an integral part of their findings. In the
following sections, we would like to review more systematically possible explanations for the sex differential
in murder and suicide. Once again, for simplicity, we
will examine these explanations under the titles used
in Chapter 2: biogenetic, psychosocial, and environmental
factors.

Biogenetic Factors

The biogenetic approach, you will remember, attempts to
examine all aspects of a biological organism from conception on. In the case of murder and suicide, there
are two major leads as to possible biogenetic involvement
that may speak to the sex differential in this area.
The first is at the chromosomal level and the second is
at the hormonal level. Very little work that examined
the biological condition of murders, suicide victims,
or attempted suicides has been done. However, if we can
agree that both murder and suicide (self murder) stem
from aggressive impulses directed either against others
or against the self, we have much broader research
results from which to draw.

Indirect support for the idea that aggression is a common
denominator in both suicide and murder may be found in
the fact that differences in aggression are among the
most consistent findings in sex difference research,
and they are in the same direction as the sex differences
we have examined in murder and suicide. According to
one recent text, sex differences in aggression are
evident as early as social play begins, at age 2 or
thereabouts, and boys show higher aggression both physically and verbally from that time on (37). While certain
circumstances can alter the level of aggression shown,
e.g., males are more affected by the presence of peers
than are females (38), the overall finding remains firmly
established. Boys and men show more aggression than do
girls and women and they do so from a very early age onward. We also find a greater male aggression among many
other species of animals (39). When we find a sex
difference across species, across cultures and from an
early age onward, we have reason to suspect some biological
involvement.

One of the first places to look for biological involvement is at the chromosomal level. Might it be possible
that the Y chromosome, which differentiates males from
females, carries information that lends itself to
greater male aggression? Intriguing, although contradictory, evidence exists which suggests this as a possibility. In 1965, a group of researchers published a
study which examined male criminals and found among them
a higher percentage of males who had an extra Y chromosome than would be expected by chance (40). Men who
have this chromosomal abnormality have a total of 47,
rather than the usual 46 chromosomes. While their
physical appearance generally seems normal and their
testosterone levels are in the normal range, XYY men
have been described as impulsive, lacking persistence,
and having a low tolerance for frustration and anxiety
(41). At least three studies, in addition to the intro-
ductory one, supported the claim that XYY males were
found more often than expected in criminal institutions
(41-43). However, there are at least three studies
which have found no increased risk of criminality among
XYY males (44-46). Several other studies done with XYY
males found that even when crimes had been committed by
these men, they were not necessarily the most violent
types of crimes, a finding which also tends to minimize
the claim that the extra Y chromosome foreordains violence.
To further complicate matters, it has been reported that
males with an extra X chromosome also have a higher
incidence of crime than would be expected by chance
alone, although they do not seem to have the same problem
with impulse control as do the XYY males (42). Since
both XYY and XXY males have higher rates of criminal
institutionalization, it would appear that if anything
is acting at the chromosomal level, it does not have a
sequential and easily predictable effect on behavior.

Moving from the chromosomal level of biology to the
hormonal level, some researchers have claimed that the
reason males have higher rates of homicide than females
is that males have higher levels of testosterone, the
chief male masculine hormone, which predisposes them
toward aggression (47). A major basis for this argument
comes from research on lower animals. Laboratory experi-
ments have shown that when male rats are castrated
immediately after birth, aggression is reduced (48) and
there is a lower incidence of pup killing (49). The
administration of testosterone to female rats neonatally
increases the incidence of pup killing (49-51). Among
female primates and sheep, at least three studies have
shown an increase in aggressive behaviors under the
influence of neonatal testosterone (52-54). If castrated
male animals receive injections of testosterone, many
of their aggressive behaviors return (48, 49). Experience
also seems to play a part in the relationship between
testosterone and aggression. One animal study showed

that male monkeys who were not dominant animals in their original situation experienced an increase in testosterone when placed with females and allowed to assume dominance. The effect was reversed when the animals were returned to the original dominance hierarchy (55). In addition, male mice and female monkeys who have had fighting experience may continue to engage in aggressive behaviors even after castration or ovarectomy, indicating that experience may offset the effect of hormones or the lack of them (56, 57).

Perhaps the foregoing is enough of a review to establish that testosterone does seem to have a strong relationship to aggressive behaviors in subhuman species. But what about in human beings? Obviously we cannot castrate males at birth or artificially masculinize females to note the effects on aggression. However, certain accidents and conditions occur in nature that allow for examination of conditions similar to those occurring with animals in the laboratory. One such condition, which changes the hormonal condition of otherwise per- fectly normal females, is known as the adrenogenital syndrome. Simply put, the adrenogenital syndrome is an inherited condition that results in masculinization of the fetus in utero. Most females so affected can be treated from birth on and can develop into normal women. Two studies of the behavior of a total of 32 such females concluded that there was a higher incidence of tomboyism among them compared to a control group (58, 59). The effect of experience with humans, however, seems to outweigh any biological bias which might be caused by such a masculinizing condition. Money and Schwartz (60) conducted a study of 15 of these androgenized females when they reached adolescence and young adulthood and found that these women did not tend toward higher aggression than did their normal peers.

The opposite type of prenatal condition also can occur; i.e., males can be feminized in utero. One way in which this may happen is when males are conceived by diabetic mothers who are treated with supplemental doses of the female hormones estrogen and/or progesterone. Yalom, Green, and Fisk (61) studied 6-year-olds and 16- year-olds so affected and found that the most consistent difference between those boys and normal boys and between those boys and boys of diabetic mothers who had not been treated with hormones was that the hormonally influenced group of boys at both ages were less aggressive.

Two cases of boys being castrated have also been reported by Money and Ehrhardt (58). In both instances, the parents chose to raise the children as females, and the children made good adjustments to their reassigned sex. Once again, these cases suggest the importance of the environment in shaping gender identity. However it is

also important to raise the question concerning the
change in the relative amount of testosterone available
to these subjects as they matured.

Examination of abnormal conditions seems to provide some
support for the fact that humans may exhibit some
behaviors that have hormonal involvement, although the
extent of hormonal effect can never be separated from
experience and learning.

In normal males, we do have some evidence, correlational
in nature, which may support the idea that testosterone
is related to aggressive behavior. In 1971, three
researchers using a technique that measured hormone
levels in the blood found a positive relationship
between testosterone level in younger males and self-
reported feelings of hostility and aggression (62). A
second study, while showing an overall lack of correlation between testosterone levels and hostility test
scores, did find two interesting correlations (63).
The first was between the testosterone level and the age
of the first conviction for a violent crime, and the
second was between testosterone level and the type of
offense committed. Men who had committed violent,
aggressive acts during adolescence had higher testosterone
levels than men who had not committed that type of
offense.

Turning to suicide, the most intriguing work relating
hormones to suicides and suicide attempts has been done
with women. Because women have a clear hormonal cycle
with peaks of estrogen and progesterone and a trough
during which both hormones diminish significantly,
researchers have attempted to correlate suicidal behaviors
with hormonal changes. MacKinnon, MacKinnon, and Thompson
found that 64 percent of the women in their sample who
committed suicide did so during the second half of the
menstrual cycle, between days 17 and 23 (64). However,
other researchers dealing with suicide attempts have
established that more attempts occur in the premenstrual
and menstrual periods (65-67). Other research done on
correlates of the menstrual cycle reveals that aggression
tends to be highest premenstrually, when both female
hormones are lowest (68, 69) and that hostility seems
to peak at this same time (70, 71). Interestingly,
Dalton reported that 49 percent of women who committed
a crime were in the premenstrual or menstrual phase of
their cycle (72). Still other researchers have attempted
to determine other physical correlates of suicide. One
researcher, Krieger (67), is illustrative. He attempted
to determine if there was a hormonal difference between
those who threatened or attempted suicide and those who
successfully completed the act at a later time. He
found a significantly higher level of blood cortisol for
13 patients who suicided within two years of the last

blood test, as compared with 39 suicide risk patients
who did not commit suicide. However, it should be noted
that much of the research in this area has been highly
criticized because of design, methodology, or bias and,
therefore, the question of biological implications either
in murder or suicide is still wide open.

It is clear that the major lines of research concerning
biological predispositions to aggression, violence, and
suicide have yielded at best only suggestive results.
Perhaps the reason lies in the nature of the human being.
In contrast to other species, humans seem to be more
open in learning through experience. Thus hormones in
humans may only predispose while the environment may
actualize violence or nonviolence. For example, XYY
males may indeed have a lower tolerance for frustration,
but if the environment is a good fit, offering a minimum
of frustration, they may never experience real problems.
Similarly, most males, because of their testosterone
levels, may have higher potential for aggression than
most females, but this may be channeled into achievement
rather than violence given a supportive environment.
Females may experience cyclic rhythms which may be
involved in suicidal or homicidal violence, but only
for those who have lived with environmental problems
for extended periods or who are reaching the end of
their tolerance for frustration. In short, there may
be different biological thresholds for eliciting violent
behaviors from men than from women and different thresholds for the same woman in different points in the cycle.
However, it is the interaction of chromosomal make-up
or hormonal levels within the individual personality and
within the psychosocial and physical environment in
which the person lives that finally determines the
nature of the act of violence.

Psychosocial Factors

Murder and suicide have long been discussed in terms of
psychological and social variables. One recent book
devotes five chapters and over 100 pages to five separate
theoretical viewpoints that fit in the psychosocial
domain: psychoanalytic theories, learning and behavioral
theories, sociological theories, ethological theories,
and sociobiological theories of aggression (8). Other
books adopt a particular stance and explain violent
behavior of the sexes according to their particular bias.
It would be impossible to review all the material
available in this section. Therefore, the discussion
has been limited to that material which seems most helpful in attempting to understand the sex differential in
murder and suicide.

The statistics examined in the first part of this chapter certainly support the notion that men live in a more violent world than do women. Why this is true is a question that psychologists and sociologists have addressed from slightly different perspectives. Earlier psychologists focused on the violence of individuals which, taken collectively, created a violent society. Thus, Lombroso and 19th-century psychologists looked at such things as the shape of people's heads and their facial features in an attempt to predict their potential for violence (73). Sociologists have tended to focus on the violence within the social milieu and to use it to predict the violence of individuals. Recently, however, both disciplines are beginning to focus on multiple aspects of the <u>interaction</u> between the individual and the society in which he is reared. The expectations of the society for males and females, the role models provided for males and females, and the reinforcers and punishers used by socialization agents are all factors that have been studied relative to the sex differential in aggression and violence.

The psychological theory that has generated a good deal of research on aggressive behaviors of the sexes is known as social learning theory. In contrast to more psychoanalytic approaches, social learning theory views the individual as essentially open to learning rather than as a victim of internal preprogrammed instincts or biological forces leading to aggression. The theorists who are best known for studying sex differences from this point of view are Mischel (74) and Bandura and Walters (75). Stressing that sex differential behavior, like all behavior, is learned, these theorists point to four mechanisms which they feel are central to this learning. They include modeling, differential reinforcement, generalization, and discrimination. Let us examine each one of these mechanisms with respect to the learning of aggression.

Modeling refers to the tendency to imitate and finally incorporate as one's own, behaviors that are observed in others. There is some evidence (76) that both children and adults attend to a same-sex more than to an opposite sex model. If this is true, then the worlds of boys and girls may be perceptually different even when they appear to be the same. For example, while two opposite-sex 4-year-old twins may be watching "Sesame Street" together, the girl may be attending to the female on the screen and modeling her behavior while the boy does the same with the male figure. This is probably adaptive for each sex as the children try to develop clearer under-standings of what it means to be a male or female. However, in terms of aggression, those same 4-year-olds watching "Hill Street Blues" may selectively model male violence and female passivity. To the extent that our

society encourages more aggressive heroes (a more popular
term for role models) for males than for females, it is
probably encouraging different levels of aggression in
the sexes. Consider the heroes of boys: generally football players, boxers, soldiers, policemen, and other
people who engage in aggressive behaviors. Compare
those with the heroes of women, which surveys have shown
to include singers, wives of politicians, tennis players,
actresses, writers, and politicians. The role models
alone suggest a basis for possible sex differences in
violence.

If boys and girls are positively reinforced or punished
for different behaviors, they are even more likely to
develop differentially. Thus, boys who are shamed for
playing with dolls may find it difficult to develop
warm, nurturing behaviors, while girls, praised for the
same behavior, will increase their play, or rehearsal,
of such behaviors. There is, however, some question
concerning the effectiveness of learning of aggression
by direct reinforcement. Maccoby and Jacklin (77) point
out that aggression may be more punished in boys than
in girls. Social learning theory predicts that consistent punishment of behaviors will lead to their
extinction. Therefore, it seems contradictory that
boys would show higher levels of aggression if they
were punished more often for aggressive acts. The key
word in explaining this contradiction may be "consistent."
While parents and teachers may indeed punish aggressive
behaviors more in boys, peers may approve and thus
reinforce the same behaviors. We all know of boys who
are regarded by teachers and other adults as "rough and
rowdy" but who are given respect and at least grudging
admiration by both their male and female classmates.
In addition, the whole business of reinforcement can be
tricky. A teacher may think she is punishing aggressive
behavior in a boy who has pushed another when she takes
him aside and scolds him. If, however, it is the only
time the teacher has spent with the boy on an individual
basis, the boy may feel reinforced rather than punished,
and may be inclined to repeat his behavior so as to get
more teacher attention. This is particularly likely to
occur if the boy has attained his goal by pushing the
other child (e.g., he gains possession of a toy the
other child wanted) or if his classmates give him
attention and/or respect as a result of his aggressive
behavior.

Girls often reinforce each other in cooperative, rather
than competitive, play. Girls jumping rope or playing
in the kitchen corner of the kindergarten are engaging
in traditional types of activities that call for verbal
interaction and sharing. These deemphasize the competition that is so often found in traditional boys'
activities, particularly organized sports.

Generalization refers to the tendency to apply a behavior
that has been reinforced to similar situations. In our
earlier example, the 4-year-old who found he could get
what he wanted by pushing will probably use this behavior
again when a similar situation arises. Discrimination
refers to the ability to use behaviors selectively.
Thus our "pushy" boy may learn by experiencing consequences that it's okay to push other 4-year-olds but not
his brother's 10-year-old friends.

The last two concepts of this theory are not terribly
helpful in explaining the sex differential in violence.
To illustrate this point, consider the findings of
several studies in modeling and reinforcement of
aggression (78-80). In these studies children were
exposed to an aggressive model or reinforced for aggressive behavior. Children of both sexes increased in
aggression. However, the boys were more aggressive than
the girls across every study. Why? If we add to social
learning theory a construct borrowed from Kohlberg's
theory (Chapter 3), we may be closer to understanding
this effect. Kohlberg, you will recall, postulates that
children are active in attempting to understand their
environments. They organize their world by creating
categories of behaviors. Thus boys, seeing more male
aggression, may conclude that to be male is to be
aggressive and act so as to conform to that understanding
even in situations in which they are not reinforced or
are actually punished. In effect, once a behavior like
aggression is incorporated into a child's self-description,
it may outweigh situational variables in establishing
behavior. Kohlberg refers to this as conformity to the
sex role. Phenomenologists have referred to this tendency to behave according to one's prior understandings
of self and the world as self-consistency (81). While
social learning theorists do not use this concept, it
does seem to be useful in helping to explain why males,
even when punished more often for aggressive behavior,
tend to act more aggressively than do girls.

The above theories tell us something about how individual
boys may come to develop higher levels of aggression
than do girls. They do not, however, tell us how the
male role first began to be associated with higher levels
of aggression. Some sociologists and ethologists have
pointed out that our gender roles have evolved over
eons of human history and often have had species survival
value. For example, young adult males have always been
expected to take the lead in hunting, fighting, and
maintaining the social order, with violence if necessary.
This allowed young adult females essential time for
pregnancy, childbirth, nursing, and rearing of human
infants, who have a relatively long dependency period.
The likelihood is that those males who were best at
aggressive defense of mate, family, and territory and

who were strongest, quickest, and least reluctant to
utilize physical violence, were those who survived to
plant their genetic traits in the next generation. Over
millennia, as this pattern repeated itself generation
by generation, males of the species might have experienced
an increasing level of strength and perhaps an accompanying predisposition toward aggression (to the extent that
aggression may have a genetic underlay). Certain
authors have maintained that the male's more frequent
participation in violence is due at least partially to
this natural selection factor (82-85).

Traditionally, the female role has been described as
one of communion (86) or expressiveness (87). Communion
is defined as a sense of "being at one with other
organisms" and is contrasted to the traditional male
role of agency which is concerned with "self-protecting,
self-expression, and self-expansion" (86, p. 15).
Expressiveness refers to the kinds of behavior that
promote harmony and stress social-emotional interactions.
It is contrasted to a male instrumental role that entails
an empahsis on tasks, goals, and the interaction between
the family unity and the larger society. It is easy to
see that these modern concepts of gender roles might be
related to the division of labor, which is believed to
have been common among early human groups. Both agency
and instrumentality would seem to permit and even encourage higher levels of aggression than would the roles
described as expressiveness and communion.

Sociologists and psychologists alike believe that poor
fit between what an individual thinks he should be (role
expectations) and what his society allows him to be,
can result in a higher incidence of aggression. Years
ago, Dollard and his associates suggested that aggression
was always a consequence of an individual's being
frustrated in satisfying some felt drive or need (88).
A detailed study done by Palmer (89) found that when
a group of murderers were compared to their nonmurdering
brothers, the level of physical and psychological frustration of the murderers was much higher. In essence,
the Palmer study found that murderous siblings were
more likely to have encountered frustrating experiences
in school, in occupations, in interpersonal relationships,
and/or with their physical health than were the nonmur-
derers. This study seemed to support the Dollard
frustration-aggression hypothesis.

Palmer (90) has also suggested that frustration can
result when an individual is unable to carry out
appropriate social roles. He refers to this inability
as "role unreciprocity" and believes that as the level
of unreciprocity increases, so does the likelihood of
other directed violence. Ketner and Humphrey (91)
carried out a study to determine, first, if murderers'

lives were characterized by higher levels of unreciprocity
compared to the lives of nonviolent criminals and, second,
if males and females experienced different levels or
kinds of unreciprocity. They found positive support for
both questions. Homicide offenders did report higher
role unreciprocity than did less violent offenders, and
four significant differences were found between males
and females in the levels of unreciprocity. Females
were found to experience "greater amounts of unrecipro-
cating events in the marital and parental roles, while
males experienced more unreciprocity in the student and
occupational roles" (91, p. 383). These findings may
illuminate the patterns in murder that we examined
earlier; i.e., females killing spouses and children and
males killing people from the outside world proportionately more often. Perhaps the old song, "You always
hurt the one you love," should be changed to "You always
hurt the one who frustrates you most."

Henry and Short (1) have stated that social changes,
particularly in the area of economics, can lead to
increased frustration and therefore increased suicide
and homicide rates. Some of their work supports the
socioeconomic differences we have seen in violent
behavior. These authors conceptualized suicide as
aggression turned inward and murder as aggression turned
outward. Because of recent changes in the status of
women in our culture, several articles have been concerned
with a possible increase in female aggression.
Steffensmeier (92) has reviewed the FBI Uniform Crime
Reports for the years 1965-1977. In the category of
violent crimes, he found that the arrest rates during
the period rose slightly both for males and for females
but he concluded, in contrast to other writers (e.g.,
93, 94), that female rates of arrests for violence had
not increased relative to males. In the thoughtful
discussion of his findings, Steffensmeier pointed out
that occupational roles are unlikely to relieve women
from their traditional domestic roles so that even as
women may find themselves with greater illegitimate as
well as legitimate opportunities outside of the home,
they will have less time and energy to engage in them
compared to men. In addition, as women increase their
earnings and match their talents to new opportunities,
their frustration levels should decrease rather than
increase. Steffensmeier also pointed out that women
still seem to disapprove more of the use of physical
force and violence than do men and that they are still
unlikely to be included in the more violent male sub-
cultures because of ingrained sex role stereotypes in
that population. It seems fair to say, based on these
statistics and observations, that in the absence of the
formation of an organized female subculture that approves
of violence as a part of a woman's role, provides violent
role models, and reinforces violent behaviors, female

rates of murder and homicide are not likely to change
drastically in comparison to those of males.

Environmental Factors

It is difficult to differentiate factors in this category
from social factors that might be included above.
However, three conditions have been suggested which
seem to be predominantly environmental rather than
psychosocial, and which may contribute to the sex
differential in murder and suicide. The first is the
availability of guns, which you will recall are used
more often by men than by women. Farley (2) has determined that the increase in homicide between 1960 and
1975 is largely due to the increase in the availability
of guns. Among nonwhite males, he maintained that the
entire increase from 419 deaths per million to 716
deaths per million resulted from additional shooting
deaths. Among nonwhite women, 90 percent of total rise
in homicide was traced to gun murders. Possession of
guns accounted for three-quarters of the total rise in
the homicide death rate while it accounted for less
than one-half of the increase among white women. Farley
found that the proportion of all homicides resulting
from gun usage increased from 55 percent in 1960 to 67
percent in 1975, and suggested that a "technological
change--a reduction in the availability of guns--would
have an even greater impact (than campaigns against
violence) upon the homicide rate" (2, p. 187). Since
many murders occur impulsively out of anger, Farley
suggests that if guns were not available, less effective
weapons might be used in the heat of the moment which
might allow for higher survival rates.

A second predominantly environmental factor is the
greater availability of drugs. More males than females
use drugs. Zahn (21) has pointed out that drug users
exist in a violent subculture and therefore are victims
of homicide or kill more often than nondrug users.

A third environmental factor can best be explained by
use of the community opportunity hypothesis proffered
by McCandless (93). McCandless has suggested that to
the extent that an environment offers legitimate
opportunities to people, they will generally avail themselves of those opportunities. When few or no legitimate opportunities exist, people will turn to illegitimate,
and riskier, activities. For females, traditionally,
legitimate opportunities have been available in
communities that denied them to males; that is, females
could always stay home and have babies, thus fulfilling
a socially approved, if not always totally satisfying,
role. In our culture, they could even expect some aid,
although rarely enough, in doing it. Men, on the other

hand, frequently have sought in vain for some external outlet for their ambitions. Although the community opportunity hypothesis has been included under environmental factors because it speaks of opportunity in the immediate environment, it clearly is related to the frustration-aggression theory and the role unreciprocity theories discussed above.

Of the three approaches to understanding the sex differential in suicide, the environmental approach is the most hopeful. For the most part it is people who create environments, and it is people who can change them. Just as lives were saved by passing a law that reduced the speed limit from 70 to 55, so also lives could be saved by passing laws restricting ownership of handguns. Local communities can take active steps to educate people about the dangers of drug usage and see to it that laws are enforced. Finally, communities can attend to the opportunities available for citizens and reorganize if necessary to promote fuller participation and decrease the frustration level of many citizens.

A POSTSCRIPT CONCERNING SUICIDE

In the theoretical discussion above, we have tended to accept the concept that suicide is aggression or violence turned inward against self while homicide represents violence or aggression turned outward against others. This chapter would not be complete, however, without a reference to Durkheim's famous classifications of suicide and an examination of their ability to account for sex differences in suicide (94).

Durkheim took a sociological view toward suicide and proposed that suicides fall into four categories that are dependent upon the degree of integration with the society which an individual experiences. His first category was called egoistic suicide and was said to occur when an individual no longer believed in the societal norms and thus saw him/herself as apart from society. The second type of suicide, anomic, was said to occur when the society lost its ability to impose regulations upon the individual. The third category, altruistic suicide, occurred when individuals over-identified with the norms of society to the extent that their lives seemed unimportant compared with the good of society and they regarded themselves as expendable. The fourth type of suicide described by Durkheim was that of fatalistic suicide. It occurred when people were victims of overly regulated societies and had no hope of realizing their life's goals or needs. One author, Johnson, reviewing Durkheim's theory with respect to why fewer women than men commit suicide, has stated that Durkheim believes that women's "traditionalism and lack of intellectuality is the reason why women can endure life--better than men" (95, p. 147). She concluded that Durkheim "considers women less socially, morally and intellectually developed than men. In fact, he draws parallels between women and 'lower societies'" (95, p. 148). Johnson did, however, find Durkheim's categories of altruistic and fatalistic suicides useful in reviewing reasons why women reported making suicide attempts. She suggested that if attempted suicides were counted along with successful suicides, the sex differential in suicidal behaviors would be equal, and she felt that classifying suicide attempts as well as successes utilizing Durkheim's schemes might shed light on the "different social worlds" inhabited by men and women. Clifton and Lee, in a series of studies examining the differential characteristics of men and women with regard to suicide, also emphasized the different social worlds of the sexes. They concluded that [while]

> women may be less prone to physical suicide, they are just as self-destructive in more passive ways. The passive position in this aspect of life is in keeping with the general passive nature of female socialization. It is consistent also with lack of confidence; little enough, in fact, to preclude active and immediate suicide and to opt instead for a decrease in life effectiveness and a waiting for something external to make the final decision (96, p. 20).

Whether suicidal women are more altruistic and fatalistic than men, as Johnson suggests, or whether they are merely more passive, as Clifton and Lee suggest, there can be no doubt that attempted suicide is a maladaptive behavior in most cases. Therefore, rather than focusing on male suicide only because it occurs more frequently, it would seem important to examine all of the factors--biological, psychological, and environmental--which go into suicidal behavior by both sexes. A culture which devotes itself to understanding why relatively large numbers of its citizens attempt to take their lives each year is likely to turn up material that will help most of its citizens cope in more healthy ways with the stress of everyday life.

SUMMARY AND CONCLUSIONS

In this chapter, we have examined the sex differential in murder and suicide. Males were found to commit murder and suicide more frequently than did females. Differences between male and female murderers were pointed out in terms of education, occupation, and nature of the crime. Victim-precipitated crimes were discussed

as were differences in suicide patterns and in attempted
suicides. Lacking definitive evidence, speculations
were made concerning the reasons for the sex differential
in homicide and suicide from three different perspectives:
the biogenetic, the psychosocial, and the environmental
perspectives. Finally, suicide and suicide attempts
were discussed from the point of view of the classic
categorization system that Durkheim proposed and its
relevance for understanding the different social worlds
of men and women today was suggested.

Murder and suicide are obviously extreme behaviors.
They are also complex behaviors, probably involving all
aspects of human experience: the biological, psychological, social, and environmental. Let us accept for a
moment the hypothesis suggested in the chapter that
chromosomal and/or hormonal biological differences between the sexes may orient boys toward more aggressive
behaviors than girls. If we then place these children
in a society that provides more violent role models for
males, lionizing aggressive heroes from football, boxing,
the army, etc., it would seem natural that boys would
accept an aggressive definition of masculinity and act
in conformity with it. In this way males in our society
may develop a self-concept with a higher level of aggression at its core than would females. Perhaps such a
self-concept was helpful, even necessary, in the past
history of the species. The question we must address
in today's society is, "Are aggressive differences
between the sexes necessary and/or helpful today?" If
the answer is no, or even perhaps not, we may want to
begin a well-organized, consistent campaign to affect
those psychosocial and environmental aspects of our
culture which might result in a decrease in the sex
differential in aggression.

REFERENCES

1. Henry, A. F., & Short, J. F. Suicide and homicide.
    Glencoe, Ill.: The Free Press, 1954.

2. Farley, R. Homicide trends in the United States.
    Demography, 1980, 17(2), 177-188.

3. U.S. National Center for Health Statistics. 1979.
    A Monthly Vital Statistical Report. August 13,
    1979, 27(13).

4. Palmer, S. The violent society. New Haven, Conn.:
    College & University Press, 1972.

5. Swigert, V. L., & Farrell, R. A. Murder, inequality
    and the law. Lexington, Mass.: Lexington Books,
    1976.

6. Wolfgang, M. Patterns in criminal homicide.
    Montauk, N.J.: Patterson Smith, 1975.

7. Lester, D. Sex differences in the homicide rate.
    Psychological Reports, 1973, 33, 250.

8. Kutash, I., Kutash, S. B., Schlesinger, L. B., et
    al. Violence: Perspectives on murder and aggression.
    San Francisco: Jossey-Bass, 1978.

9. Allen, N. H. Homicide: perspectives on prevention.
    New York: Human Sciences, 1980.

10. Houts, M. They asked for death. New York: Cowles,
    1970.

11. Resnick, P. Child murder by parents. American
    Journal of Psychiatry, 1969, 126, 325-334.

12. Resnick, P. J. Murder of the newborn: A psychiatric
    review of neonaticide. American Journal of Psychi-
    atry, 1970, 126, 1414-1420.

13. Myers, S. Maternal felicide. American Journal of
    Disabilities of Children, 1979, 120, 534-536.

14. Rasko, G. The victim of the female killer.
    Victimology, 1976, 1, 396-402.

15. Totman, J. The Murderess. Police: July-August,
    1971.

16. Eysenck, S., & Eysenck, H. The personality of
    female prisoners. British Journal of Psychiatry,
    1973, 122, 693-698.

17. Cole, K., Fisher, G., & Cole, S. Women who kill.
    Archives of General Psychiatry, 1968, 19, 1-8.

18. Russell, D. E. H., & Van de Ven, N. Crimes against
    women: Proceedings of the international tribunal.
    Millbrae, Calif.: les femmes, 1976.

19. Schafer, S. Victimology: The victim and his
    criminal. Reston, Va.: Reston Publishing, 1977.

20. Palmer, S. Sex differences in criminal homicide
    and suicide in England and Wales and the United
    States. Omega, 1980-81, 11, 255-270.

21. Zahn, M. A. The female homicide victim, Criminology,
    1975, 13, 400-415.

22. Gove, W. R. Sex, marital status and suicide.
    Journal of Health and Social Behavior, 1972, 13,
    204-213.

23. Wexler, L., Weissman, M., & Kasl, S. Suicide
     attempts 1970-75: Updating a United States study
     & comparison with international trends. British
     Journal of Psychiatry, 1978, 132, 180-185.

24. Marks, A. Sex differences and their effect upon
     cultural evaluations of methods of self-destruction.
     Omega, 1977, 8, 65-70.

25. Lester, D. Why people kill themselves. Springfield,
     Ill.: Charles C Thomas, 1972.

26. Diggory, J. C., & Rothman, D. Z. Values destroyed
     by death. Journal of Abnormal Social Pscyhology,
     1961, 63, 205-210.

27. Newman, J. F., Whittemore, K. R., & Newman, H. G.
     Women in the labor force and suicide. Social
     Problems, 1973, 21, 220-230.

28. Diamond, H. Suicide by women professionals.
     Dissertation Abstracts International, 1978, 38(10-B),
     5009-5010.

29. Pitts, F., Schuller, A., Rich, C., & Pitts, A.
     Suicide among U.S. women physicians 1967-1972.
     American Journal of Psychiatry, 1979, 136, 694-696.

30. Schaar, K. Suicide rate high among women psychol-
     ogists. APA Monitor, 1974, 5(7), 1.

31. Taylor, M. Sex and suicide: A study of female
     labor force participation & its effect upon rates
     of suicide. Dissertation Abstracts International,
     1978, 39(5-A), 3168.

32. Gove, W. R., & Tucker, J. F. Adult sex roles and
     mental illness. American Journal of Sociology,
     1973, 78, 812-835.

33. Radloff, L. Sex differences in depression: The
     effects of occupation and marital status. Sex
     Roles, 1975, 1, 249-265.

34. Jacobson, G. F., & Portuges, S. H. Relation of
     marital separation and divorce to suicide: A
     report. Suicide and Life Threatening Behavior,
     1978, 8(4), 217-224.

35. Herman, S. Women divorce and suicide. Journal of
     Divorce, 1977, 1(2), 107-117.

36. Wenz, F. O. Suicide and marital status: A case of
     high suicide rates among the widowed. Crisis
     Intervention, 1976, 7(4), 149-161.

37.   Unger, R. K. Female and male psychological perspec-
      tives. New York: Harper & Row, 1979.

38.   Maccoby, E. E., & Jacklin, C. N. The psychology
      of sex differences, Stanford, Calif.: Stanford
      University Press, 1974.

39.   Hoyenga, K. B., & Hoyenga, K. T. The question of
      sex differences. Boston: Little, Brown, 1979.

40.   Jacobs, P. A., Brunton, M., Melville, M. M.,
      Brittain, R. P., & McClemont, W. F. Aggressive
      behavior, mental subnormality and the XYY male.
      Nature, 1965, 208, 1351-1352.

41.   Nielson, J., & Christensen, A. Thirty-five males
      with double Y chromosomes. Journal of Psychological
      Medicine, 1974, 4, 38-47.

42.   Hook, E. B. Behavior implications of the human XYY
      genotype. Science, 1973, 179, 139-150.

43.   Price, W. H., Brunton, M., Buckton, K., & Jacobs,
      P. A. Chromosome survey of new patients admitted
      to the four maximum security hospitals in the
      United Kingdom. Clinical Genetics, 1976, 9, 389-398.

44.   Kessler, S., & Moos, R. H. The XYY karyotype and
      criminality: A review. Journal of Psychiatric
      Research, 1970, 7, 153-170.

45.   Jacobs, P. A., Price, W. H., Richmond, S., &
      Ratcliffe, R. A. Chromosomal surveys in penal
      institutions and approved schools. Journal of
      Medical Genetics, 1971, 8, 49-58.

46.   Owen, D. R. The 47 XYY male: A review. Psychological
      Bulletin, 1972, 78, 209-233.

47.   Persky, H., Smith, K. D., & Basu, G. K. Relation
      of psychologic measures of aggression and hostility
      to testosterone production in man. Psychosomatic
      Medicine, 1971, 33, 265-277.

48.   Baenninger, R. Effects of day 1 castration on
      aggressive behaviors of rats. Bulletin of the
      Psychonomic Society, 1974, 3, 189-190.

49.   Rosenberg, K. M., & Sherman, G. F. Testosterone
      induced pup-killing behavior in the ovariectomized
      female rat. Physiology and Behavior, 1974, 13,
      697-699.

50.   Rosenberg, K. M., & Sherman, G. F. The role of
      testosterone in the organization, maintenance and

activation of pup-killing behavior in the male rat.
Hormones and Behavior, 1975, 6, 173-179.

51. Rosenberg, K. M., & Sherman, G. F. Influence of
    testosterone on pup killing in the rat as modified
    by prior experience. Physiology and Behavior,
    1975, 13, 669-672.

52. Goy, R. W. Early hormonal influences on the devel-
    opment of sexual and sex-related behavior. In F.
    O. Schmitt (Ed.), The neurosciences second study
    program, pp. 199-207. New York: Rockefeller Univer-
    sity Press, 1970.

53. Eaton, G. G., Goy, R. W., & Phoenix, C. H. Effects
    of testosterone treatment in adulthood on sexual
    behavior of female pseudohermaphrodite rhesus
    monkeys. Nature, New Biology, 1973, 242, 119-120.

54. Clarke, I. J. The sexual behavior of prenatally
    androgenized ewes observed in the field. Journal
    of Reproductive Fertility, 1977, 49, 311-315.

55. Williams, J. Psychology of women: Behavior in a
    biosocial context. New York: Norton, 1977.

56. Herman, B. H., & Hyde, J. S. Effects of chronic
    testosterone administration on fighting behavior
    in adult female wild mice genetically selected for
    differences in aggression. Paper presented at the
    meeting of the Midwestern Psychological Association,
    Chicago, May 1976.

57. Vom Saal, F. S., Svare, B., & Gandelman, R. Time
    of neonatal androgen exposure influences length of
    testosterone treatment required to induce aggression
    in adult male and female mice. Behavioral Biology,
    1976, 17, 391-397.

58. Money, J., & Ehrhardt, A. A. Man and woman, boy
    and girl. Baltimore: Johns Hopkins University
    Press, 1972.

59. Ehrhardt, A. A. Prenatal hormonal exposure and
    psychosocial differentiation. In E. J. Sachar (Ed.),
    Topics in psychoendocrinology, pp. 67-82. New York:
    Grune & Stratton, 1975.

60. Money, J., & Schwartz, M. Fetal androgens in the
    early treated adrenogenital syndrome of 46, XX
    hermaphroditism: Influence on assertive and
    aggressive types of behavior. Aggressive Behavior,
    1976, 2, 19-30.

61. Yalom, I. D., Green, L., & Fisk, N. Prenatal

exposure to female hormones. Archives of General Psychiatry, 1973, 28, 554-561.

62. Persky, H., Smith, K., & Basu, G. Relation of psychologic measures of aggression and hostility to testosterone production in man. Psychosomatic Medicine, 1971, 33, 265-277.

63. Krenz, L. E., & Rose, R. G. Assessment of aggressive behavior and plasmo testosterone in a young criminal population. Psychosomatic Medicine, 1972, 34, 321-332.

64. MacKinnon, I. L., MacKinnon, P. C. B., & Thompson, A. D. Lethal hazards of the luteal phase of the menstrual cycle. British Medical Journal, 1959, 1, 1015-1017.

65. Sommer, B. Menstrual cycle changes and intellectual performance. Psychosomatic Medicine, 1972, 34, 263-269.

66. Smith, S. L. Mood and the menstrual cycle. In E. J. Sachar (Ed.), Topics in psychoendocrinology, pp. 19-58. New York: Grune & Stratton, 1975.

67. Krieger, G. Is there a biochemical predictor of suicide? Suicide, 1975, 5, 228-231.

68. Morton, J. H., Addison, H., Addison, R. G., Hunt, L., & Sullivan, J. A. A clinical study of premenstrual tension. American Journal of Obstetrics and Gynecology, 1953, 65, 1182-1191.

69. Silbergeld, S., Brast, N., & Noble, E. B. The menstrual cycle: A double-blind study of symptoms, mood, and behavior, and biochemical variables using Enovid and placebo. Psychosomatic Medicine, 1971, 33, 411-428.

70. Paige, K. E. Effects of oral contraceptives on affective fluctuations associated with the menstrual cycle. Psychosomatic Medicine, 1971, 33, 515-537.

71. Bardwick, J. M. Psychology of women. New York: Harper & Row, 1971.

72. Dalton, K. The premenstrual syndrome. Springfield, Ill.: Thomas, 1964.

73. Lombroso, C. Crime, its causes and remedies. Boston: Little, Brown, 1911.

74. Mischel, W. A social-learning view of sex differences in behavior. In E. E. Maccoby (Ed.), The develop-

ment of sex differences. Stanford, Calif.: Stanford
University Press, 1956.

75. Bandura, A., & Walters, R. H. Social learning and
      personality development. New York: Holt, Rinehart
      & Winston, 1963.

76. Slaby, R. G., & Frey, K. S. Development of gender
      constancy and selective attention to same-sex models.
      Child Development, 1975, 46, 849-856.

77. Maccoby, E. E., & Jacklin, C. N. The psychology
      of sex differences. Stanford, Calif.: Stanford
      University Press, 1974.

78. Bandura, A., Ross, D., & Ross, J. Imitation of
      film-mediated aggressive models. Journal of
      Abnormal and Social Psychology, 1963, 66, 3-11.

79. Bandura, A., Ross, P., & Ross, S. Vicarious
      reinforcement and imitative learning. Journal of
      Abnormal and Social Psychology, 1963, 67, 601-607.

80. Bandura, A. Influence of models' reinforcement
      contingencies on the acquisition of imitative
      responses. Personality and Social Psychology,
      1965, 1, 589-595.

81. Lecky, P. Self consistency: A theory of personal-
      ity. Fort Myers Beach, Fla.: Island Press, 1973.

82. Audrey, R. The territorial imperative. New York:
      Atheneum, 1967.

83. Morris, D. The naked ape. New York: McGraw-Hill,
      1967.

84. Lorenz, K. On aggression, New York: Harcourt Brace
      Jovanovich, 1966.

85. Storr, A. Human aggression. New York: Atheneum,
      1968.

86. Bakan, D. The duality of human existence: Isolation
      and communion in western men. Chicago: Rand McNally,
      1966.

87. Parsons, T., & Bales, R. F. Family, socialization
      and interaction process. New York: Free Press,
      1953.

88. Dollard, J., Miller, N., Doob, L., Mowrer, O. H.,
      & Sears, R. Frustration and aggression. New
      Haven: Yale University Press, 1939.

89. Palmer, S. A study of murder. New York: Crowell,
     1960.

90. Palmer, S. Deviance and conformity. New Haven:
     College and University Press, 1970.

91. Ketner, L. G., & Humphrey, J. A. Homicide, Sex
     role differences and role relationships. Omega,
     1977-1980, 10(4), 379-387.

92. Steffensmeier, D. J. Sex differences in patterns
     of adult crime, 1965-77: A review and assessment.
     Social Forces, 1980, 58(4).

93. McCandless, B. R. Adolescents: behavior and devel-
     ment. Hinsdale, Ill.: Dryden, 1970.

94. Durkheim, E. Suicide. (1897, J. A. Spaulding and
     G. Simpson, trans.) New York: Free Press, 1951.

95. Johnson, K. K. Durkheim revisited: "Why do women
     kill themselves?" Suicide and Life Threatening
     Behavior, 1979, 9(3), 145-153.

96. Clifton, A. K., & Lee, D. E. Self-destructive
     consequences of sex-role socialization. Suicide
     and Life Threatening Behavior, 1976, 6, 11-22.

THE EXPERIENCE
OF BEREAVEMENT
AND GRIEF

Give sorrow words. The grief that does not speak
Whispers the o'er-fraught heart, and bids it break.

Shakespeare, <u>Macbeth</u>

INTRODUCTION

Jeanine Smith is killed in an auto accident, leaving her
husband of 18 years and two adolescent children. Jim
Smith, her husband, feels immediate shock, bewilderment,
and a sense of unreality. With the help of friends and
the funeral director, he arranges for a visitation at
the funeral home, a church memorial service, and a
graveside prayer service. Although he attends all three
of these services with his sons, he later confesses he
has little or no memory of the details; that he felt
like "he was seeing everything through a screen or a
veil."

When the ceremonies are over, Jim arranges to take two
weeks off from work and spends most of the time in bed
or drinking. On Monday of the third week, he appears
in the office and reassumes his duties without a word
to anyone concerning his loss. Within two weeks co-
workers begin to forget Jim's wife's death and assume
that he is the same person he always was. Neighbors
and friends stop bringing food and volunteering to wash
clothes and straighten the house. Jim and his sons
begin to redistribute the home tasks and to formulate a
new routine. To an external observer Jim is making a
rapid and healthy adjustment to his loss.

Internally, however, Jim is feeling a variety of turbulent
emotions: anger at his wife for not avoiding the accident

111

and at himself for not being with her; more prosaic anger
at her for leaving him alone to finish raising the children; loneliness; confusion over the new demands involved
in being both mother and father; inadequacy over domestic
details such as cooking and cleaning; regret over some
things he did and some he did not do while Jeanine was
living; depression over losing a real part of his past
identity; sadness concerning the loss of future dreams
of what might have been; and fear that he will not be
able to adjust and "be strong" for the children. Jim
feels a real need to talk out some of his feelings but
realizes that the only person he really has been able to
share with during the past two decades is Jeanine. This
thought increases his desolate feelings of loss and
starts the whole cycle over again.

Jim's case is typical in many ways of the pattern of
bereavement and loss in our culture and times. Bereavement, according to the dictionary, is the state of being
left desolate or saddened by loss. In Jim's case,
bereavement started at the moment he was informed of
Jeanine's death. Grief is the complex process that
follows bereavement and takes time and energy to
work through. Jim's varying emotions and constant sense
of depression and loss are typical of the grief process.
Mourning consists of the observable elements of grief,
which in Jim's case are at a minimum. The visitation,
funeral, and memorial service are the only real aspects
of mourning that Jim observed.

Mourning customs are generally taught by society and may
reveal a great deal about how the society views death.
In our modern society, it is almost possible to take the
dead out of the picture. Acceptable customs allow for
rapid disposal of the body and little or nothing in the
way of a memorial service. It is almost as though we are
saying that death is not a part of life or that it is
too private or embarrassing to develop overt customs for
the bereaved. Some people maintain that the elimination
of observable signs of bereavement (e.g., black armbands
for men, black clothing for women, wreaths or black
ribbons on the door of the deceased's home, etc.) help
life to get back to normal more quickly and at least
outwardly this would appear to be true. But where does
a man like Jim, who prides himself on his male strength,
go to express his feelings? And how does he let people
know that he is still hurting and at risk three weeks
after the death or three months afterwards? Our society
has not been very sensitive in providing outlets for
grieving in the recent past. We have, however, begun to
do studies on the effects of grief on physical and mental
health. Such research may prove helpful in raising our
awareness of and ability to deal with the needs of the
bereaved.

RESEARCH ON THE EXPERIENCE OF GRIEF

Grief is a universal experience. Some writers have
claimed that grief is not solely a human response.
Certain animal species do seem to express almost human
symptoms of grief when their mate or offspring dies.
For example, jackdaws and geese who have lost a mate
frequently engage in searching and calling behavior,
followed by a period of depressed activity (1). Such
behaviors seem to parallel those of infants who have
lost their main caretaker. Bowlby's classic work on
grief and mourning in infancy has suggested that even
very young children, 6 months and beyond, go through a
process of mourning when they lose their main caretaker
and that this process is intimately related to separation
anxiety (2). Bowlby described the stages of infant
grief as consisting of protest, despair, and apathy, a
sequence which seems to parallel the searching and
calling behavior of birds, followed by depressed level
of activity. Infant grief can be so severe that the
child's withdrawal will be complete and he or she will
eventually die.

Stages of grief appear to be a normal part of all human
grief reactions. Although they are called by different
names by different researchers, they essentially consist
of an initial reaction of shock, disbelief, despair,
and despondency followed by a gradual period of recovery
and then by a time of reinvestment. In an early article
describing the grief process, Lindemann (3) interviewed
and summarized the reactions of 100 people who had lost
family members in a large restaurant fire. He reported
that all of the people experienced wavelike somatic
symptoms consisting of "a feeling of tightness in the
throat, choking with shortness of breath, need for sigh-
ing, and an empty feeling in abdomen, lack of muscular
power and an intense subjective distress described as
tension or mental pain" (p. 147). After a review of
the literature on the effects of death, Parkes concluded
that "bereavement can affect physical health, and that
complaints of somatic anxiety symptoms, headaches,
digestive upsets and rheumatism, are likely, particularly
in widows and widowers in middle age" (4, p. 341). In
addition, he pointed out that certain potentially fatal
physical ailments, including coronary thrombosis, blood
cancers, and cancer of the neck and womb may be related
to recent losses.

The fact that both males and females are affected by
grief can perhaps best be illustrated by the results of
the following three studies. A 1963 study of widowers
over the age of 54 found an increase of almost 40% in
their death rate during the first six months after
bereavement, a figure far in excess of chance (5). In
1968, researchers in Australia published a study conducted

with widows under the age of 60.   Twenty-eight percent
of the sample of widows reported deterioration in health,
compared to only 4.5 percent of a married control group
(6).   A 1970 study that followed widows throughout the
first year after bereavement concluded that, regardless
of age, women whose spouses have died are more likely to
die themselves or to be emotionally or physically ill
than are married women (7).   The literature on grief is
replete with studies that support the notion that bereavement leaves the survivors, males and females, at higher
risk for both morbidity and mortality.

In addition to the general grief reaction following
bereavement discussed above, there are at least two other
types of situations in which grief is experienced.   The
first occurs when a person is confronting his or her own
death and can best be called preparatory grief.   The
process of preparatory grief is at least as painful as
the grief process following death.   While the loss of a
loved one is extremely painful, a person who is dying is
about to lose everything he or she loves: all relationships, interests, material objects as well as the most
devastating loss of all, loss of self.   Kübler-Ross has
described the grief process involved in preparatory grief
as comprising five different stages: denial, anger,
bargaining, despair/depression, and acceptance (8).   Her
formulation of these stages has been criticized as being
too "pat" and has sometimes been misused by caregivers who
believe them to be prescriptive rather than descriptive
in nature.   Nevertheless, her formulation of the stages
grew out of intensive work with terminally ill patients
and seems to be a subdivision of the three stages of
grief mentioned above that other researchers have found.

A second type, anticipatory grief, occurs when one is
awaiting the death of a loved one.   Research with parents
of dying children has indicated that if there is a
period of at least four months in which parents can prepare themselves for the loss, parents are able to accept
the child's death with more calmness and less physical
symptomology than if the time is shorter (9).   In this
grief reaction, parents work through much of the grief
process prior to the death of the child.   Anticipatory
grief seems to follow the general grief response but has
been described in different terms.   The five stages of
anticipatory grief include acknowledgment of the inevitability of death, grieving, reconciliation or coming to
grips with the reality and attempting to find meaning in
the illness and death, detachment or the gradual withdrawal of emotional investment in the dying person, and
finally, memorialization or the idealizing of the dying
person so as to create a mental image that will live
beyond the death (10).   Anticipatory grief does not seem
to be any less painful than grief that occurs following
bereavement, but it does seem to leave the person less
damaged immediately following the death.

The experience of grief is not only universal; it is
unavoidable. The only ways by which people could hope
to avoid grief is if they died before everyone else for
whom they cared or if they systematically chose not to
care for anyone. Neither of these alternatives seems
very attractive. In addition, even if the choice to
die first were made, the person choosing would have to
die quickly, as in an accident, in order to avoid
suffering preparatory grief. For most of us, then,
grief, like death, is a part of life. We have already
pointed out that both males and females experience grief.
The remainder of this chapter will examine, within the
framework of a life-span perspective, grief situations
in which males and females may have different levels of
energy investment, or different concerns, problems, or
reactions. It is not the purpose of this chapter to
determine if males are more damaged by loss and grief
than are females or vice-versa, but rather to review what
is known concerning the process of grief as experienced
by males and females in our culture.

FOR WOMEN ONLY?

The biological ability of women to conceive and bear a
child and to nurse that child is a powerful force shaping
life-style, personality, vocational choice, etc.,
especially during young adulthood. While it obviously
takes both a male and a female to begin a pregnancy,
the female alone can choose to end it. The legalization
of abortion is a relatively new development in our
culture, but it has already generated a good deal of
research just as spontaneous abortion (miscarriage) has
done. Abortion, whether it is viewed as the purposeful
taking of a human life or just the disposal of a potential
human being, is a death-related loss. Even when most
welcomed, abortion represents the decision to terminate
one set of possibilities and thus involves loss. In
this section, we will review some of the research concerning the effects of both types of abortion, spontaneous
and therapeutic, on females and the little existing
research found that included males.

A 1978 article suggested that at least 5 percent of
unmarried female college students became pregnant every
year (11). This figure, combined with those for high
school and junior high school students as well as the
figure for mature women who, married or unmarried, opt
for abortion, resulted in a 1978 annual abortion rate of
417 abortions for every 1,000 live births, according to
the Statistical Abstract of the U.S.: 1980, 101st edition
(24). Most of the literature concerning therapeutic or
induced abortions indicates that there is a low incidence
of psychological and/or physical complications among
healthy women (e.g. 12-19). However, the literature

does suggest that after abortion many women feel a
transient syndrome that has been called the "abortion
hangover" or "post-abortion blues." It consists of
feelings of anger, depression, and anxiety, self-reproach,
and guilt, all emotions that are evident in normal
grieving processes. Since abortion is physically stressful, involving the sudden termination of a host of hormonal processes as well as anesthesia and surgical insult
to the body, it is realistic to expect at least a small
degree of reaction. On top of the physical trauma,
there is the psychological stress to the woman of making
a hard decision and perhaps violating some of her early
teachings and beliefs in the process. In addition, it
is probably the rare woman who, upon discovering that
she is pregnant, does not fantasize about the baby and
her potential mothering relationship with it at least
for a brief period. Therefore, some feeling of loss is
probably involved in most abortions. This may be
balanced by a sense of relief at having an unexpected
problem resolved, but it nevertheless takes energy to
work through feelings engendered by an abortion.

While coping with stress and loss may be a neutral
experience or may even produce growth in the long run,
it may also be a precipitating factor in psychopathology,
especially in women who have a history of poor coping
or depression (20). At least two authors have pointed
out that in our haste toward validating a woman's right
to make decisions concerning her own body, we may run
the risk of overlooking some women who may need help in
dealing with the psychological trauma involved in an
induced or therapeutic abortion (20, 21).

The weight of available evidence also indicates that
there is a temporary but perhaps more severe grief
reaction for most women after a spontaneous abortion.
Spontaneous abortion is more clearly a grief-related
phenomenon as it involves unexpected and generally
unwanted termination of pregnancy. Corney and Horton
cited a Danish study that reported that 15 percent of
Danish women studied complained of "nervous symptoms"
following a spontaneous abortion (22). They compared
these figures to an American study that found that two-
thirds of the sample reported feeling depressed and/or
disappointed following spontaneous abortion. Three of
the 32 women in the American study continued to be
significantly depressed more than a year after the
abortion. Corney and Horton suggest that such depression
may be an instance of pathological grief, and they go on
to describe a patient whose symptoms were resolved by
the use of grief therapy techniques.

In contrast to women seeking abortion, who may have
worked through ambivalent feelings, women who suffer a
spontaneous abortion seem to have a very real need to

deal with the loss and to grieve for at least a short
period of time. One woman, after spontaneously aborting
her second pregnancy, expressed her feelings in the
following poem:

Lament for a Lost Child

Jan Morton

She's gone, like false dawn's glorious glow
This child that I will never know
And time cannot completely heal
the depth of loneliness I feel
and hunger, like a burning pain
to know the essence once again
of feeling life within;
Not any life, but this one lost,
this child, whose total gift and cost
was three short months of fight towards birth
Who might, perhaps, have changed the earth,
or brushed the tiny, tearful eye
of her own children, bye and bye.
She's gone, like twilight's ghostly gray
fades into blackness, killing the day.

Women choosing to abort may well have worked through
much of their feelings of loss before the abortion just
as people anticipating a death are able to work through
much of their grief before the actual bereavement. Women
who spontaneously abort, on the other hand, must deal
with their grief after the fact. The great majority of
women in both categories are able to cope with their
loss in a healthy fashion. Certain factors in the
history of the woman, however, may make her a higher
risk for a prolonged grief reaction. Such factors might
include ambivalent feelings about the pregnancy, a
history of deaths in the family with unresolved grief
feelings, a history of psychopathology, strong religious
feelings about the sanctity of life and high levels of
stress, anxiety, and/or guilt (20, 21). In summary,
although they seem to be in the minority, there are women
in both the induced and the spontaneous abortion categories
who may need help in dealing with the loss which abortion
represents, and the techniques involved in grief therapy
are probably most appropriate to this situation.

While there may be conflicting opinions about the extent
of loss felt when an abortion occurs, the same is not
true in the case of women who lose newborn infants. In
1977, the United States was 14th among nations in terms
of infant mortality (23). There were approximately 13.8
deaths for every 1,000 live births in the U.S. during
1978 (24). That figure includes a rate of 12.1 deaths
per 1,000 births among whites and 21.1 deaths per 1,000
births among blacks, reflecting once again the same racial

bias we saw in the homicide and overall death rates.
Once again, we find the now familiar sex differential
in mortality, as male infants have an excessive risk of
neonatal death compared to females. In a study of 2,735
consecutive newborn autopsies, the author concluded that
"removal from the maternal environment reveals an independent underlying male disadvantage which is conspicuous
in life within the first 72 hours of postnatal life in a
wide variety of disorders" (25, p. 905).

Mothers' reactions to the death of their newborns are
definite grief reactions. One study conducted by Kennell,
Slyter, and Klaus showed that of 18 mothers whose newborn (usually premature deliveries) had died, all 18
reported "definite sadness and preoccupation with thoughts
of the dead baby; all but two experienced insomnia and a
disturbance of their usual patterns of daily life" (26,
p. 346). Other symptoms reported included increased
irritability for 15 of the 18 and loss of appetite for 12
of the 18 women. The authors of this study also talked
to eight of the husbands of the women in their sample,
although this was not a planned part of the study. Only
two of the husbands denied grieving, giving the rationale
that they had to be strong for their wives' sake. Several
of the husbands showed as much grief or more than their
wives, particularly those husbands who had had contact
with the baby after birth. The authors of the study concluded that mourning was present in every mother in the
study, regardless of the length of the pregnancy or the
conditions surrounding the baby's birth and death as
well as in most of the fathers. Because this is true,
the authors suggested that "a substantial degree of
affectional bonding precedes tactile contact between
mother and infant" (26, p. 348). They noted the need
for both parents to be advised to express their feelings
concerning the loss of the baby and placed special
attention on the father since our culture tends not to
focus on his reaction as much as on that of the mother.
A second study also reported that all of the mothers
and most of the fathers showed a high degree of mourning,
although they handled it differently (27). Mothers
tended to grieve for a longer period and to express more
guilt and yearning for a physical presence to rock and
hold, while fathers felt they were expected to act strong
and deny feelings of grief, especially to friends and
other family members. Fathers did seem to progress
faster in the resolution of their grief than did mothers,
pehaps because they had more regular and routine contact
with an outside world, which seems to discourage and
ignore expressions of grief.

In an article written for nurses, Sylvia Bruce advises
nurses to be attentive to the particular loss which a
mother feels. She pointed out that irrational guilt
feelings are common among mothers after a stillbirth and

that empathy, recognition of feelings, and verbal as
well as tactile reassurances are part of the nurses'
arsenal for helping the mother cope with grief. Nurses
also need to be able to handle hostility, anger, and
aggression in a receptive way, Bruce pointed out, since
these are normal parts of the grief experience. Bruce's
mothers seemed to stress the element of loss above all.
One, echoing some of the sentiment of the poem cited
earlier, said: "I got so mad and upset whenever anyone
told me I was lucky, as I had two children at home, and
time to have more....I didn't care if I had a house full
of them or could have 20 more. This baby was important
at the moment, not the ones I had, or could have, but
this one. I don't think anyone even understood" (28,
p. 89). Another mother of a stillborn baby said, "It's
like losing a part of myself. Even if you have never
seen them, you do love them" (29, p. 2028).

A DEATH IN THE FAMILY

If such grief is felt at the loss of a newborn with whom
there are few past associations and shared experiences,
it is easy to understand the grief reaction of parents
to the deaths of older babies and children. We will
examine sudden infant death syndrome (SIDS), which
represents perhaps the most dramatic type of death among
young babies. It claims 8,000 to 10,000 lives a year in
the United States and has been the object of a good bit
of research since 1974, when Congress passed legislation
that called for autopsies, data collection, family counseling, and public information on the subject (30).

In spite of the fact that the cause of sudden infant
death is unknown and that the deaths are totally unpre-
dictable, occurring in seemingly healthy infants, intense
feelings of guilt are the most common reaction to this
type of death. Lee Salk has described the problems of
the surviving family members when a baby dies of SIDS:
"There may be an all-pervasive grief, an absolute disbelief in what has happened, an intense panic, a feeling
of helplessness, a wish to die, or feelings of deperson-
alization with a strong need for reality testing to prevent
further emotional and cognitive disequilibrium" (31, p.
249). Both parents experience grief and guilt. One
study indicated that parents agreed that SIDS was the
most severe crisis they had ever faced and that it took,
on the average, 15.9 months for them to regain feelings
of personal happiness they had achieved before the death
(32). The prevalence of guilt reactions among parents
of SIDS children reflects the parents' recognition of
failure in one of the most important functions of parent-
hood, that of protection of the young.

While the mother may wonder what she could have done to
avoid the death, the father may feel his very identity
as a person threatened. Gyulay has pointed out that
American society places a heavy load on men's shoulders
(33). They are never allowed to fail without feeling
guilt and shame. Failure to keep a child safe and
healthy is perhaps the ultimate failure. This, coupled
with the fact that the father is often left physically
as well as psychologically alone as relatives and friends
try to help the mother and remaining children, may serve
to make the father feel that his only use is to cope with
the bills and business matters surrounding the death;
that his grief is not important.

Siblings also need help in the case of sudden infant
death, especially if they are too young to understand
fully the meaning of death. Jealousy and accompanying
anger are often present among children. When a child
dies, sometimes the young siblings may feel guilty either
because they wished the child dead or because they feel
relieved of a burden of competition by the child's death.
Cain, Fash, and Erickson found that living children
experienced disturbed reactions in the form of both guilt
and feelings of responsibility when a sibling died (34).
Some reacted by becoming depressed and/or withdrawn.
Others became behavior problems following a sibling death.

One mother, whose 2-year-old son died suddenly, shared
the reaction of her 4-year-old daughter. As she began
to tell Sarah of her brother's death, the 4-year-old
backed away from her until she was standing in the fire-
place. With wide eyes and trembling voice, she shook her
head and said over and over, "I didn't do it, Mommy, I
didn't do it."

Obviously, siblings of children who die need time and
attention as well as needing to be included and informed
about the realities of their sibling's death at a level
which they can understand. (See Chapter 3 for stages of
children's understanding of death, and Chapter 6 for
approaches to death education.) Parents who attempt
to shield remaining children by sending them away to
relatives or friends after the death or using euphemisms
like, "Your brother has gone to sleep," may be planting
the seeds for later disturbance. Even though very young
children may not fully understand the permanence and
inevitability of death, they need to be encouraged to
express their fears, their anger, and their guilt and
to ask questions which may help to avert feelings of
isolation and self-hatred. Often the realities of death
are less frightening than the fantasies experienced by
the young child in the absence of fact. In addition,
the support children feel when things are explained to
them helps them to continue on a positive level of trust.

Some evidence exists that bereavement in childhood may have later consequences on mental health and longevity. While much of this research is poorly designed and should therefore be considered as merely suggestive, it is interesting and is important in its implications for dealing with children who have suffered a death in the family. As long ago as 1927, Abraham suggested that the death of a parent might predispose the child in later life to depressive illnesses (35). At least two studies have found support for this hypothesis. One found that 41 percent of a sample of 216 depressed adult patients had experienced the death of a parent before the age of 15 (36). A second found that 27 percent of 100 patients who had been classified as "high depressed" had lost a parent before the age of 16 compared to only 12 percent of patients in the nondepressed group (37). One article, which reviewed the evidence concerning childhood bereavement and later mental health problems, cited six studies that found higher than anticipated rates of childhood bereavement among schizophrenic patients while five studies showed no relationship. The authors of the review carried out their own study, which compared a group of adults (average age = 33) who had been bereaved as children with a group of adults whose childhood homes had been broken by divorce, and a third group of adults coming from unbroken homes. They concluded that "childhood bereavement is a serious personal crisis that can have serious consequences for later adult life" (38, p. 57). They did, however, state that children from divorced homes fared at least as poorly as those from homes broken by death. Finally, they pointed out that a "normalizing" effect seemed to occur over the years which helped to deemphasize the traumatic effects of parent loss. Other studies have found a greater incidence of patients institutionalized for a variety of reasons who have experienced parental death as children (39-43). Furthermore, at least one study seemed to indicate that the earlier the death of the parent, the more likely it is that there may be a subsequent problem (43). Most of these studies have not been directed toward examining their data by sex. However, two different studies have suggested that women who lost a parent while they were between the ages of 10 and 14 may be predisposed to suicide in later life (44, 45).

A third study, designed to determine the effect of a father's death during latency, interviewed 19 women who had suffered such a loss (46). The women felt that the death of their father had had a very significant effect on their lives. In later life they attributed conflict in male-female relationships, feelings of insecurity, dependence, and depression as well as other difficulties to this loss. While some of this attribution may be a rationalization of normal problems, it is still interesting to observe that the women felt that their father's

death had causal impact on their lives. Another study
found that daughters of widows were more inhibited, rigid,
and restrained around males than were daughters of
divorcees (47). The author also found that early separation from fathers had more serious effects than late
separation.

There is, of course, no direct cause-effect relationship
between experiencing a death and later poor mental health.
The key to the effect death will have on a child is the
quality of coping the child can do or is helped to do at
the time of the death. As Moss and Moss pointed out,
"early childhood separation is a bitter, lasting lesson
in the transiency and the finitude of life. The child
is jolted into awareness of a fact that many adults
learn only gradually; relationships are not permanent;
they change and they can be severed" (48, p. 192).
According to Erikson, perhaps our best-known life span
psychologist, the early years of life are spent attaining
a sense of trust (49). Early losses may greatly hamper
the formation of a healthy sense of trust, while the way
a child copes or fails to cope with the loss may establish
patterns for coping with the inevitable losses of later
life. All children need help in establishing healthy
coping techniques. Parness emphasized this point by
stating that "avoidance or denial of sadness and/or
anger may become a source of distortion and mystifica-
tion..." (50, p. 6). Too often, survivors may urge
children, especially boy children, not to show their
grief; to be the "man of the house" or "mama's little
man." It may well be that boys, particularly from age
10 on, need special help in coping with death. In addition to the expected reaction to loss--sorrow, anger,
bewilderment, and the like--the young boy may have the
additional burden of stoicism thrust upon him. He may
feel ashamed to show his grief, yet in some way guilty
for not showing it. He may need permission to verbalize
anxiety, fear, and sorrow as he may view these as
"feminine" emotions. In short, he may need even more
help than his sister in finding healthy ways to cope
with grief.

ADULT GRIEF REACTIONS

A wealth of literature exists on the subject of adult
grief reactions, much of it dealing with the area of
widowhood. Research on the widowed frequently includes
sex differences or detailed descriptions of reactions of
one sex which can then be compared to detailed descriptions
of the other sex carried out in other studies. Before
we begin to examine this research, however, we will look
briefly at other losses which adults may experience.

Birtchnell, in a series of studies investigating the
effect of parent death on adult children, reported the
following: significantly more adults admitted to mental
hospitals had experienced the death of a parent within
the previous five years than would be expected by chance;
significantly more of the severely depressed compared to
the moderately depressed had experienced the recent
death of a parent, and people who attempted suicide had
experienced significantly more recent parent deaths than
those who had not attempted suicide (51-53). Furthermore, Birtchnell found that for his entire sample the
recent death of a father was a significant precursor of
mental illness, while the recent death of a mother was
not. Looking only at depressed men patients, however, he
found that recent death of their mother was a significant
factor. In the United States, three researchers interviewed 14 adults whose parent(s) had died within the
past three to 20 months (54). They pointed out that
"death of a parent marks the end of one's oldest relationship and affects one's relationships with survivors. The
confrontation with death and aloneness may catapult a
person into a period of profound soul-searching and
existential crisis" (54, p. 1155). While their data are
based on a small sample size, the clinical implications
they draw from it are thought-provoking. They believe
that therapists working with bereaved adults must attempt
to determine what personal meaning the death of a parent
represents. Often the meanings are not obvious even to
the mourner. The death of a parent may mean to some
adult children that they now represent the oldest (and
wisest?) generation. It may mean added responsibility
for some as they assume the role of the real head of
the family. For some, it may bring the sure knowledge
that the end of an era of unquestioned and unearned
acceptance and love has come to an end. For others, it
may mean that unresolved conflicts and childhood anger
and resentment can now never be resolved.

Sanders (55), in a larger study, compared the reactions
of 102 adults who had recently lost either a child, a
spouse, or a parent with those of a nonbereaved control
group. She, like many others, found more physiological
symptoms among her total bereaved group than among the
controls. Of the three situations, the death of a child,
whether very young or middle-aged, produced the highest
intensity grief reaction. This finding provides support
for Gorer's earlier description of the loss of an adult
child as perhaps the most distressing and long-lasting
of all griefs (56). Women who had lost spouses reported
significantly more physical problems and higher death
anxiety than did males who had lost their spouses. The
death of a parent evoked the lowest intensity of grief
reaction among the adults in this study. Sanders did
not find support for the fact that anticipating a death
lessens the intensity of the grief process.

ABOUT WIDOWHOOD

By far the most prolific area of research about death with
adults is that of the loss of a spouse. According to a
1977 study, over 700,000 of the 30,000,000 people over 50 in
the United States lose a spouse each year (57). There
are more than 10 million widows in the United States;
three out of every four married women will be widowed
at one time or another. One out of every 20 people in
1977 was either a widow or a widower (58).

The widowed research frequently contrasts males and
females so that sex differences in widowhood are more
available than in other areas of death research. In
fact, there are two schools of thought concerning spouse
bereavement in adulthood. The first may be said to be
represented by Parkes, who made the statement that "one
way or another women usually come out of bereavement
worse than men" (59, p. 123). The second is that men,
because they are less prepared to cope with the everyday
necessities of domestic life, e.g., planning nutritious
meals, cooking, shopping wisely, chauffeuring children
to myriad functions, etc. are hardest hit by widowhood.
The truth is that like so many other areas, generalizations regarding which sex has the most problem in widowhood are probably incorrect. Among the pertinent
questions that must be asked in any spouse bereavement
situation are the following: Which widow(er)? How old
is (s)he? What are the survivor's financial and family
obligations and what support systems are available? How
long has it been since the death occurred? What functions
did the deceased mate fulfill for the survivor and what
was the quality of the relationship? Was the death
anticipated or sudden? What skills does the bereaved
have in social, vocational, and interpersonal areas
which will help him/her reenter the mainstream of life
after bereavement? Widowhood is a complex condition,
and simple answers or generalizations are bound to mis-
represent any given individual situation.

One major factor to be considered in any study of widowhood is that of age. Several studies have confined
themselves to working with older survivors or younger
survivors only. A few studies have contrasted both
young and old widowed persons. Perhaps the best review
of prospective studies comparing different ages was done
by Paula Clayton (60). She concluded that widows and
widowers of all ages report suffering from significant
depressive symptoms during the first year after bereavement. Younger widows and widowers, however, seem to
experience more physical distress and tend to take more
drugs than do the older bereaved persons. Older men
seem to experience an increase in mortality during the
first year of bereavement while this was not true in the
studies she reviewed for younger men or for women at any

age. The amount of psychiatric care does not seem to
increase for widows during the first year. Clayton concluded that although death of a spouse is a psychologically
stressful event accompanied by a great number of psychological symptoms, generally both widows and widowers
seem to handle their grief well regardless of age (with
the possible exception of elderly males).

Not all studies are as sanguine regarding adjustment to
bereavement as is Clayton's. One of the earliest of
many studies of the widowed (61) was referred to at the
beginning of this chapter. The sample consisted of nearly
5,000 Welsh widowers who were 50 years of age or older.
They were followed for nine years after their wives'
deaths in 1957. Of the sample, 213 died during the first
six months of bereavement. This is a figure 40 percent
above that expected for married men of the same age.

The Welsh study supported a 1967 study that examined
903 bereaved relatives who exhibited a 4.76 percent
mortality rate during the first year of bereavement
compared to a 0.68 percent mortality rate in a matched
control group (62). Although not all of those who died
were spouses, the majority were.

In a recent review of the literature on the mortality of
bereavement, Jacobs and Ostfeld (63) found that the
risk of mortality among the bereaved might be as high as
50 percent. They found that younger persons and men
were at higher risk of death during bereavement. They
also noted that the first six months after bereavement
were the most dangerous for men, while the second year
after bereavement seemed more difficult for women. Men,
for the first half year after the death of their wives,
showed an excess of deaths from suicide, accident, and
disease of the heart. Women, during that same period,
showed a higher risk of diseases of the heart followed
by a higher risk of cancer during the second six months.
Overall, however, women were at lower risk for death than
men. Jacobs and Ostfeld concluded that there is a basic
pattern of excess mortality especially in males among
the bereaved. Their review seems to support the wisdom
of the old folk stories that bereaved people can "die of
a broken heart."

Short of fatality, loss of spouse can also have profound
effects on the physical and psychological health of the
survivor. Toynbee has pointed out that there are always
"two parties to the suffering that death inflicts; and,
in the apportionment of this suffering, the survivor
takes the brunt" (64). The well-known Harvard study
examined bereaved men and women under 45 years of age
and compared them 14 months after bereavement with nonbereaved subjects of the same age. They found a host of
significant psychological, physical, and behavioral

differences between the groups (65, see Appendix for
details). Not only did the bereaved in this study report
more hospital admissions and consult with more people
concerning emotional problems, they also reported more
problems in the areas of sleeping and eating and an
increase in consumption of drugs such as tranquilizers
and alcohol. They reported, among other psychological
symptoms, feelings of depression, restlessness, poor
memory, indecision, loneliness, and anxiety. When a
score of one for each physical symptom that the respondents
reported had occurred for the first time in the year
following bereavement was given, widowers showed a
significant increase in symptoms while widows did not,
in comparison with the control group.

Psychologically, however, widowers may fare better than
do widows. In a study of 78 widows and 41 widowers who
were interviewed 13 to 16 months after bereavement,
Carey found that the widowers were significantly better
adjusted than were the widows even if such factors as
level of income, level of education, age, and amount of
forewarning of death were considered (66). Carey suggested three reasons for this differential: (1) Women,
at least in the past, have been conditioned to build
their identities around their husbands while the same
is not true of the men in our culture. A good illustration is the almost universal practice in our culture of
taking the man's name in marriage, thereby symbolically
giving up the earlier independent identity. (2) Since
men die earlier than women and since surviving men tend
to marry younger women, there is less likelihood that
women will remarry; widows, knowing this, feel less hope
for future intimacy than do widowers. (3) Widows voiced
their concern about making decisions and handling finances
alone, as well as concern for their physical safety and
worry about their children. Widowers tended to report
concern over handling the physical and emotional needs
of children alone and over the details involved in
maintaining their homes. Carey suggested that the concerns of the widows outweighed those of the widowers.
This study, as is true of others, found that widows who
had forewarning of the deaths of their husbands (at
least two weeks) made better adjustments. Forewarning
was not a significant factor for males. Younger widows
were less well adjusted than older widows, while those
who were more highly educated and earned more money
were better adjusted. Thus age, forewarning of death,
and education level seemed important variables in
mediating adjustment to bereavement.

More than 20 years ago, Cumming and Henry suggested that
widowhood was less difficult for women in the United
States than was retirement for men (67). Their rationale
had to do with the fact that there were many other widows
with whom to share leisure time and activities so that a

widowed woman's status actually increases while a retired
man's status decreases. Lopata (68) disagreed with this
observation and went on to conduct a study in which she
interviewed more than 300 widows over 50 years of age in
the Chicago area. Based on this and other work, Lopata
reported that our society, like many others, has not
addressed the problem of the social isolation of widows.
She stated that the social isolation that many widows
experience is a result of having removed "women's
ascribed social relations or at least those relations
achieved early in life, while not making other ones
available to them or training them to enter new social
roles voluntarily" (68, p. 45). She went on to explain
that in our increasingly mobile society, kin groups have
broken down and that, particularly for the elderly
widowed, no substitute for extended families has been
forthcoming. Since older women have also received
strong socialization pressures to be passive, it was
not surprising to note that the widows in her study
listed loneliness as their chief problem. Lopata stated
that her studies indicated that "the social isolation
of the widow is basically related to a lack of competence
in the development and maintenance of social relations,
rather than to a voluntaristic disengagement" (68, p.
45). In a later article, Lopata reported that education
and social class play a major role in the way in which
a widowed woman reconstructs her identity and her world
after the death of her husband (69). She believed that
poorer, less educated women defined themselves more in
terms of their relation to their children than to their
husband, while more highly educated, wealthier women
identified more with their husband's career, health
status, etc. Both relative wealth and education increase
alternatives available for readjustment. Thus, higher
income, better educated women appear to be affected more
by widowhood but are at the same time more capable of
rebuilding a satisfying life. Middle-class educated
widows, Lopata concluded, need little or no societal
help in adjusting to widowhood since they have the where-
withal to enter new roles and make new lives. Indeed,
she found that many widows reported feeling stronger,
freer, and more independent as a result of working their
way through the bereavement process. However, some of
the widows whom Lopata studied shared a multifaceted
profile which indicated that readjustment after widowhood
might be difficult, if not impossible. Lopata eloquently
described their plight: "They are women in a male dominated
society. They are old in a society that venerates youth.
Many are grieving and lonely in a country that would deny
and ignore such unhappy emotions. They are without mates
in a social network of couples. Many are members of
ethnic or racial minority groups and already face pre-
judice on that basis. ...They are poor in a wealthy
land and they tend to be ignorant and uneducated in a
society that increasingly demands knowledge and skills"
(69, p. 92).

Other studies of widows have focused on younger widows
and the set of problems they face, particularly if they
have young children at home. Conroy (70), for example,
pointed out that in addition to having to cope with the
psychological and physical stress of bereavement,
younger women frequently had to adjust to drastic changes
in financial status, particularly if the husband was the
main wage earner and insurance was minimal, as is
common with many younger couples. For example, the
young widowed mother must frequently take on the instrumental role that her husband used to play. She must
leave home to find work or be reeducated so that she
may enlarge her work options. Frequently, a move is
necessitated, either because of her return to work or
school, or because she can no longer afford to maintain
the family home. Sometimes young widows move in order
to be close to family members who can help in the rearing
of the children. Whatever the reason, moving on top of
being widowed presents another source of loss. Frequently, young widows find that they cannot develop a
new social life even when the grief process begins to
subside because they have little time or energy left
over after trying to be both mother and father to their
children--earning the money, paying the bills, helping
children with homework, cleaning the house, cooking the
meals, etc. In addition, many traditionally reared
women find it difficult to take the initiative in building new social relationships even if time and energy
permitted. Sometimes, young widows may find to their
horror that they are developing resentment toward their
children since their presence keeps the widow from re-
suming her earlier single life-style and may also be a
factor in preventing remarriage. This resentment breeds
guilt and presents yet another source of emotional
upheaval in the life of the young widow.

Schlesinger, in an article concerning widowhood in
Canada, supported Lopata's observations by reporting
that problems faced by the widow and her family fall
into three main categories: economic, social, and
emotional (71). Canadian society, he maintained, with
its emphasis on individualism and independence, provides
only minimal support for a bereaved family once the
funeral ceremony is over. Therefore, death of a husband
frequently results in family disorganization in Canada
as well as in the United States. Another Canadian
study, this one conducted with 100 widows under 69 years
of age, revealed that the younger women in the population
(those under 45) reported experiencing more stress than
did the older widows. Those who were living with their
children also reported significantly higher levels of
stress than those who lived alone or who lived with
their children and another adult such as their mothers
(72). Augmenting higher stress levels among younger
widows is the fact that two-thirds of the women with

children at home noted that the children were having
difficulty adjusting to their father's death. Thus,
younger widows with children faced a myriad of personal
economic, psychological, and social problems and also
had to deal with their dependent children's complex of
similar problems. This study had one other interesting
finding that tended to support the notion that anticipatory grief may alleviate some of the more acute
bereavement symptoms. Just as parents of terminally ill
children seemed to be able to face their loss with more
equanimity if they had had at least four months to prepare for it, the widows in this study reported experiencing
more stress if their husbands had had a fatal illness of
less than two months compared to those widows whose
husband's final illness was one year or more in length.

In a study designed to test whether age and/or time for
anticipatory grieving would make a difference in the
intensity of the grief reaction, Ball discovered that
young widows (under 46 years of age) experienced a
stronger grief reaction than did middle-aged or elderly
widows regardless of the suddenness of death of their
husbands (73). However, across all groups, deaths which
did not allow for anticipatory grieving evoked stronger
grief reactions. In comparison with middle-aged and
older widows, the younger widows seemed to profit more
from having a period of anticipatory grief. Ball concluded that age is a more important factor than mode of
death (sudden as compared to prolonged) in mitigating
the grief response. Greenblatt reiterated these findings,
claiming that at least three separate authors have shown
that intense grief lasts longer in those who experience
sudden loss and that this is particularly true for young
widows (74).

While middle-aged and older widows seem to have fewer
problems in coping with certain aspects of grief, there
are considerations that complicate the picture in a
different way than is true for the young widow. The
middle-aged and the elderly generally have a sense of
limited time, which is not true for the younger widow.
Thus, while the young widowed mother may feel overwhelmed,
she is also likely to feel that when she gets things
sorted out, she will be able to choose among a variety
of futures. She may choose further schooling, a new
type of job, or to remarry. Middle-aged women frequently
feel it is too late for them to go back to school and
that the odds are against them finding another mate.
These feelings are often even stronger among the elderly
widowed. In addition, both the middle-aged and the
elderly cohort were raised at a time when there was more
of a division of labor in the home than may be the case
for today's young widow. As Lynn Caine and others have
pointed out, many widows don't know where the circuit
breakers are located in their homes, have never changed

a fuse, can't mow the lawn, and don't know a thing about
the motor of their automobile (75). Becoming a widow
during mid-life or beyond frequently means having to
acquire a whole set of skills for which one has no prior
socialization and little motivation. Complicating
matters even more, even when these widows are able to
find work outside of the home, it frequently is not a
major source of identity for them as it is for many men
(76).

The adjustment of elderly widows to the loss of their
spouse seems to be mediated to a great extent by their
other social support systems. One study showed that
contacts with friends and neighbors were positively
related to lower levels of loneliness and worry and to
higher feelings of usefulness among a large group of
elderly widows (77). Indeed, at least in this study,
relationships with nonrelatives were more important to
successful adjustment than within-family relationships.
The author discussed this as a result of the fact that
friendships are generally based on common interests and
life-styles, while the concern of family members may be
out of duty only. Family relationships may also threaten
the widowed elderly, in that they may contain some
elements of role reversal between the middle-aged child
and the aging parent and may suggest or demand dependency
from the elderly.

A study examining the level of disengagement among
elderly persons found that the major cause of separation
from society was the loss of a spouse (78). It further
found that those who had become disengaged from society
generally had low morale. Widowed elderly with few
supportive relationships, therefore, probably have the
poorest prognosis for readjustment after bereavement.

While younger widows seem to profit from having some time
for anticipatory grieving, the same does not seem to be
true for elderly widowed. In a study conducted with 81
widows and widowers, the researchers found that the aged
bereaved (mean age = 67) whose spouse died of a lengthy,
chronic illness did worse than did the bereaved whose
spouses died after short-term illnesses (79). In addition,
in this study male survivors whose spouses had a chronic
fatal illness showed more physical symptoms than did
female survivors. The authors suggest that "the period
of anticipatory grief is dysfunctional for the aged male
bereaved" (p. 227). The authors discuss their findings
in light of the fact that elderly persons may have health
problems which they neglect in caring for their dying
spouse. They may also find the experience lonely as they
cut off ties to the outside world while they engage in a
lengthy death watch. Unless support is given to aged
spouses, they may emerge from a prolonged experience of
helping their mates to die with fewer social ties than

they previously had and with less physical and emotional
energy to invest in working through the grief process
and reinvesting in new relationships. Males may find
themselves at a particular disadvantage during a lengthy
dying process in that their socialization prohibits them
from asking for help, showing strain, or even, in some
instances, recognizing and discussing their feelings with
helping professionals.

Not all studies of bereavement and the elderly yield such
negative findings, however. One prospective study, begun
in 1955 by researchers at Duke University, tested a small
group of elderly (males mean age = 74.8; females = 73.1)
21 months after the death of their spouse (80). The
subjects had received an extensive set of medical, psychological, and laboratory examinations at the time of
initial contact some years before the death occurred and
had lived together until one spouse died. The initial
set of examinations was repeated 21 months after bereavement. The researchers reported that the lives of elderly
bereaved were not characterized by social disintegration.
They found little or no health deterioration in their
sample. They did find a small but significant decline
in work, usefulness, and total attitude scores with a
greater decline in work attitude scores for men and in
usefulness scores for women. Their overall conclusions
were that the elderly of both sexes "adapt to the death
of a spouse in a fashion characterized by (1) emotional
stability, (2) stable social network, (3) few life
changes, and (4) only time-related health deterioration"
(p. 359). In this sample, the elderly seemed to prepare
themselves for widowhood by gradual identification with
the role before the actual event and seemed to gain a
great deal of strength from religious supports.

One emotion that has not been discussed thus far is that
of relief. In a series of interviews conducted with
widows and widowers in preparation for this chapter, the
emotion of relief was often mentioned. One widow who was
discussing her immediate reaction to her husband's death
after a lengthy respiratory illness said, "It wasn't a
suprise, but it's always a shock when somebody dies."
Then she said, "I went over and patted him because he
looked so nice and relaxed" in a tone of voice that
implied, "This death was all right." Another widow, after
explaining that her artist husband had not been able to
use his hands for the last weeks prior to his death,
explained, "It was a relief when I knew that there was no
chance of him being better. ...It was a great relief
because he was so unhappy. ...At first, I felt very
thankful that the suffering that he had endured for so
long was over."

A widower, whose wife of 47 years died of complications
surrounding rheumatoid arthritis, expressed his feelings

this way: "I felt it was a merciful thing she passed on because of the way she was suffering. I had asked God to take her. I didn't want her to keep suffering. Of course, I was upset after she did go but I was thankful for it too." He went on to discuss feelings of emptiness and loneliness during the next few months, but the relief he felt at the cessation of suffering seemed to moderate the worst of the grief experience.

Another widower said, "At first my reaction was a sense of relief because I didn't want her to suffer. I didn't want her to die, but I didn't want her to suffer. If she couldn't get well, I wanted her to die with dignity."

Toynbee has pointed out that "if one truly loves a fellow human being, one ought to wish that as little as possible of the pain of his or her death shall be suffered by him or her and that as much of it as possible shall be borne by oneself" (64, p. 331). However, he went on to say that while most people can wish this with their minds, it is almost impossible to wish it with their hearts. Therefore, a bereaved person who feels relief at the death of a suffering loved one, will still have grief work to perform.

SUMMARY AND DISCUSSION

Death is a major stress-producing situation in the lives of all people. Bereavement, grief, and mourning customs tend to be played down in our society. However, grieving, like illness brought on by other causes, cannot be denied. It will be experienced. Both males and females experience the same kind of symptoms connected with grief. These include sleep and appetite disturbances, feelings of nervousness, anxiety, depression, crying spells, "pangs" of loss, remorse, and loneliness, and increase in physical symptoms, and fatigue and reduced working capacity. In general, the grieving process includes three phases: one of shock and disbelief, one of despair and despondency, and one of gradual recovery and reinvestment of energy.

The necessity to experience and work through grief accompanies every loss, including therapeutic and spontaneous abortions. There is evidence that both parents of stillborn children and sudden infant death syndrome victims need to grieve, and that the father may well need added permission to vent his grief. This may well be true for all traditionally reared males beyond the age of 10 as they attempt to deal with loss. However, both male and female children who experience death may be at risk for later psychological disturbance if the grief process is not satisfactorily resolved. Further, although the evidence is conflicting, males seem to react with more physical symptomology leading to an increase in illness

and death during the first year following bereavement,
while females seem to experience a higher incidence of
psychological symptoms. Enough studies have shown that
both males and females are "at risk" for pathology after
a death to encourage a concerned society to be aware of
the need and be prepared to provide assistance to the
survivor-victims for a period of up to two years following
the loss.

A major factor that must be considered in any attempt to
understand the widowed is that of age. Younger widows
seem to be harder hit by grief than are older widows but
may well have the best prognosis for working through their
grief to a satisfactory resolution, all other things being
equal. Younger widows seem to make a more rapid adjustment to bereavement if they have had some forewarning of
the death. This does not seem to be true either for
widowers or for older widows. Indeed, for elderly widows
and widowers alike, lengthy illnesses of their spouses
seem to be related to poor bereavement outcomes. Other
factors that have been shown to affect the outcome of
bereavement include income, educational level, and amount
of religiosity (with the last factor being particularly
important with elderly populations).

There is an apparent contradiction in the literature
concerning widowers. More of them develop physical
symptoms and die during the first six months of bereavement than is true for widows. However, more widowers
than widows seem to make adequate or good adjustments to
bereavement. This apparent contradiction might be understood in light of the heightened mortality risk of males
in general. The shock of bereavement may cause death
more frequently in males than in females simply because
of a relative biological weakness. However, it may also
be that males may be more inclined than females to express
the shock and depression following a death in life-
threatening ways such as excessive drinking, driving when
drunk, speeding in cars, excessive smoking, etc. Bock
and Webber (81) found the suicide rates of elderly widowers
to be significantly higher than those of married men,
married women, and widows. If widowers do survive the
first six months to a year after bereavement, our society
is so structured that males may be more easily able to
reconstruct their lives in a positive way, thus exhibiting
better adjustment than do females. At least the younger
widowers have jobs as a major source of their identity
and are expected to take the initiative in forming new
relationships. Also, they are often sought out socially
in a society where women outnumber men, while widows may
be viewed as adding an awkward burden to the social
situation. Kastenbaum suggests that widowers may make
faster social recoveries than do widows but slower
emotional recoveries since they view expression of grief
as weak or unmasculine (82).

Although grief is mainly a negative experience, it may also be accompanied by feelings of relief, particularly if the deceased suffered for a long period of time or if the survivors were beginning to feel overstressed physically, emotionally, or financially because of the terminal illness. While feelings of relief may make the initial response to death easier, they do not negate the necessity of working through the grief process.

As people in our society become more open to the study and discussion of the subject of death, we may find that it is easier to relate to the bereaved. Certainly, as we come to recognize the components of grief and the fact that the process of grief is an individual one which cannot be speeded up, we may be able to offer support over a longer period to bereaved persons. Such support may be different for men than for women. Women may need help with such practical things as fixing the washing machine or learning to handle finances. Men may need help with other types of practical things such as planning nutritious meals and learning how to follow a recipe. Women may need a sympathetic ear to listen to them. Men may need both a sympathetic ear and a sense of psychological permission to vent their feelings and to appear emotionally dependent for a time. However, both sexes share in common the need for strength to face the loneliness, depression, and hopelessness which the loss of a loved one entails.

REFERENCES

1. Averill, J. R. Grief: Its nature and significance Psychological Bulletin, 1968, 70, 721-798.

2. Bowlby, J. Grief and mourning in infancy and early childhood. Psychoanalytic Study of the Child, 1960, 15, 9-52.

3. Lindemann, E. Symptomatology and management of acute grief. American Journal of Psychiatry, 1944, 101, 141-148.

4. Parkes, C. M. The broken heart. In Shneidman, E. S. (Ed.), Death: current perspectives, p. 333-347. Palo Alto: Mayfield, 1976.

5. Young, M., Benjamin, B., & Wallis, C. Mortality of widowers. Lancet, 1963, 2, 454-456.

6. Maddison, D., & Viola, A. The health of widows in the year following bereavement. Journal of Psychosomatic Research, 1968, 12, 297-306.

7. Parkes, C. M. The first year of bereavement: A longitudinal study of the reaction of London widows

to the death of their husbands. Psychiatry, 1970, 33, 444-467.

8. Kübler-Ross, E. On death and dying. New York: Macmillan, 1969.

9. Natterson, J. M., & Knudson, A. G. Observations concerning fear of death in fatally ill children and their mothers. Psychosomatic medicine, 1960, 23, 456-465.

10. Stillion, J. M., & Wass, H. Children and death. In Wass, H. (Ed.), Dying: Facing the facts. Washington: Hemisphere, 1979.

11. Rader, G. E., Bekker, L. D., Brown, L., & Richardt, C. Psychological correlates of unwanted pregnancy. Journal of Abnormal Psychology, 1978, 87, 373-376.

12. Patt, S. L., Rappaport, R. G., & Barglow, P. Follow-up of therapeutic abortion. Archives of General Psychiatry, 1969, 20, 408-411.

13. Senay, E. Therapeutic abortion: Clinical aspects. Archives of General Psychiatry, 1970, 23, 408-415.

14. Pohlman, E. Abortion dogmas needing research scrutiny. In Sloane, A. Abortion: Changing views and practice. New York: Grune & Stratton, 1971.

15. Osofsky, J. D., & Osofsky, H. J. The psychological reactions of patients to legalized abortion. American Journal of Orthopsychiatry, 1972, 42, 48-60.

16. Ewing, J. A., & Rouse, B. A. Therapeutic abortion and a prior psychiatric history. American Journal of Psychiatry, 1973, 130, 37-40.

17. Werman, D. S., & Raft, D. Some psychiatric problems related to therapeutic abortion. North Carolina Medical Journal, 1973, 34, 274-275.

18. Hrari, M. B. Abortion. In Freedman, Kaplan, & Sadock (Eds.), Comprehensive textbook of psychiatry, vol. 11. Baltimore: Williams & Wilkins, 1975.

19. Lask, B. Short-term psychiatric sequelae to therapeutic termination of pregnancy. British Journal of Psychiatry, 1975, 126, 173-177.

20. Mester, R. Induced abortion and psychotherapy. Psychother. Psychosom., 1978, 30, 98-104.

21. Spaulding, J. G., & Cavenar, J. O. Psychoses following therapeutic abortion. American Journal of Psychiatry, 1978, 135, 364-365.

22. Corney, R. T., & Horton, F. T. Pathological grief
     following spontaneous abortion. American Journal of
     Psychiatry, 1974, 131, 825-827.

23. United Nations. Demographic Yearbook, 1978. New
     York: United Nations, 1979.

24. U.S. Bureau of Census. Statistical Abstract of the
     United States: 1980. 101st edition, Washington,
     D.C.

25. Naeyem, R. L., Burt, L. S., Wright, D. L., Blanc,
     W. A., & Tatter, D. Neonatal mortality, the male
     disadvantage. Pediatrics, 1971, 48, 902-906.

26. Kennell, J. H., Slyter, H., & Klaus, M. H. The
     mourning response to the death of a newborn infant.
     The New England Journal of Medicine, 1970, 283,
     344-349.

27. Helmrath, T. A., & Steinitz, E. M. Death of an
     infant: Parental grieving and the failure of social
     support. The Journal of Family Practice, 1978, 6,
     785-790.

28. Bruce, S. J. Reactions of nurses and mothers to
     stillbirths. Nursing Outlook, 1962, 10, 88-91.

29. Seitz, P. M. & Warrick, L. H. Perinatal death: The
     grieving mother. American Journal of Nursing, 1974,
     74, 2028-2033.

30. Nakushian, J. M. Restoring parents' equilibrium
     after sudden infant death. American Journal of
     Nursing, 1976, 76, 1600-1604.

31. Salk, L. Sudden infant death: Impact on family and
     physician. Clinical Pediatrics, 1971, 10, 248-250.

32. DeFrain, J. D., & Ernst, L. The psychological
     effects of sudden infant death syndrome on surviving
     family members. The Journal of Family Practice,
     1978, 6, 985-989.

33. Gyulay, J. The forgotten grievers. American
     Journal of Nursing, 1975, 75, 1476-1479.

34. Cain, A. C., Fash, I., & Erickson, M. Z. Children's
     disturbed reactions to the death of a sibling.
     American Journal of Orthopsychiatry, 1964, 34, 741-
     752.

35. Abraham, K. Selected papers of Karl Abraham.
     London: Hogarth, 1927.

36. Brown, F. Depression and childhood bereavement. Journal of Mental Science, 1961, 107, 754-777.

37. Beck, A. T., Sethi, B. B., & Tuthill, R. W. Child-bereavement and adult depression. Archives of General Psychiatry, 1963, 9, 129-136.

38. Bendiksen, R., & Fullon, R. Death and the child: An auterospective test of the childhood bereavement and later behavior disorder hypothesis. Omega, 1975, 6, 45-60.

39. Barry, H. Significance of maternal bereavement before the age of eight in psychiatric patients. Archives of Neurology and Psychiatry, 1949, 62, 630-637.

40. Parkes, C. M. The effects of 1964 bereavement on physical and mental health: A study of the medical record of widows. British Medical Journal, 1964, 2, 274-279.

41. Granville-Grossman, K. L. Early bereavement and schizophrenia. British Journal of Psychiatry, 1966, 112, 1027.

42. Stein, Z., & Susser, M. Widowhood and mental illness. British Journal of Preventive Social Medicine, 1969, 23, 106-110.

43. Birtchnell, J. Early parent death and mental illness. British Journal of Psychiatry, 1970, 116, 281-288.

44. Greer, S., Gunn, J. C., & Kaller, K. M. Aetiological factors in attempted suicide. British Medical Journal, 1966, 2, 1352-1355.

45. Hill, O. W. Child bereavement and adult psychiatric disturbance. Journal of Psychosomatic Research, 1972, 16, 357-360.

46. Henrichs, M. H. Daughters' responses to paternal bereavement: A study of women who were latency age when their fathers died. Dissertation Abstracts International, 1978, 4032-B.

47. Hetherington, E. M. Effects of father absence on personality development in adolescent daughters. Developmental Psychology, 1972, 7, 313-326.

48. Moss, S. Z., & Moss, M. S. Separation as a death experience. Child Psychiatry and Human Development, 1973, 3, 187-194.

49. Erikson, E. H. Childhood and Society (2nd ed.). New York: Norton, 1963.

50. Parness, E. Effects of experience with loss and death among pre-schoolers. Children Today, (Nov.-Dec.) 1975, 2-7.

51. Birtchnell, J. Depression in relation to early and recent parent death. British Journal of Psychiatry, 1970, 116, 299-306.

52. Birtchnell, J. The relationship between attempted suicide, depression and parent death. British Journal of Psychiatry, 1970, 116, 307-313.

53. Birtchnell, J. Psychiatric breakdown following recent parent death. British Journal of Medical Psychology, 1975, 48, 379-390.

54. Malinak, D. P., Hoyt, M. F., & Patterson, V. Adult reactions to the death of a parent: A preliminary study. American Journal of Psychiatry, 1979, 136, 1152-1156.

55. Sanders, C. M. A comparison of adult bereavement in the death of a spouse, child and parent. Omega, 1979-1980, 10, 303-322.

56. Gorer, G. Death, grief and mourning in contemporary Britain. London: Cresset, 1965.

57. Jacobs, S., & Ostfeld, A. An epidemiological review of the mortality of bereavement. Psychosomatic Medicine, 1977, 39, 344-357.

58. Conroy, R. C. Widows and widowhood. New York State Journal of Medicine, 1977, 77, 357-360.

59. Parkes, C. M. Bereavement: Studies of grief in adult life. International Universities Press, 1972.

60. Clayton, P. The sequelae and non-sequelae of conjugal bereavement. American Journal of Psychiatry, 1979, 136, 1530-1534.

61. Parkes, C. M., Benjamin, B., & Fitzgerald, R. G. Broken heart: A statistical study of increased mortality among widowers. British Medical Journal, 1969, 1, 740-743.

62. Rees, W. D., & Lutkins, S. G. Mortality of bereavement. British Medical Journal, 1967, 4, 13-16.

63. Jacobs, S., & Ostfeld, A. An epidemiological review of the mortality of bereavement. Psychosomatic Medicine, 1977, 39, 344-357.

64. Toynbee, A. The relation between life and death,
    living and dying. In E. Schneidman (Ed.), Death:
    Current perspectives. Palo Alto: Mayfield, 1976.

65. Parkes, C. M. Studies of grief in adult life. New
    York: International Universities Press, 1972.

66. Carey, R. G. Weathering widowhood: Problems and
    adjustments of the widowed during the first year.
    Omega, 1979-80, 10, 163-173.

67. Cumming, E., & Henry, W. Growing old. New York:
    Basic Books, 1961.

68. Lopata, H. Z. The social involvement of American
    widows. American Behavioral Scientist, 1970, 14,
    41-58.

69. Lopata, H. Z. Living through widowhood. Psychology
    Today, July 1973, 87-92.

70. Conroy, R. C. Widows and widowhood. New York State
    Journal of Medicine, 1977, 77, 357-360.

71. Schlesinger, B. The crisis of widowhood in the
    family cycle. Essence, 1977, 1, 147-155.

72. Vachon, M., Formo, A., Freedman, K., Lyall, W.,
    Rogers, J., & Freeman, S. Stress reactions to
    bereavement. Essence, 1976, 1, 23-33.

73. Ball, J. F. Widows grief: The impact of age and mode
    of death. Omega, 1976-77, 7, 307-333.

74. Greenblatt, M. The grieving spouse. American Journal
    of Psychiatry, 1978, 135, 43-47.

75. Caine, L. Widow. New York: William Morrow, 1974.

76. Resnick, J. L. Women and aging. The Counseling
    Psychologist, 1979, 8, 29-30.

77. Arling, G. The elderly widow and her family,
    neighbors and friends. Journal of Marriage and the
    Family, 1976, 38, 757-768.

78. Brown, A. S. The elderly widowed and their patterns
    of social participation and disengagement. Disser-
    tation Abstracts International, 1972, 422-A.

79. Gerber, I., Rusalem, R., Hannon, N., Battin, D., &
    Arkin, A. Anticipatory grief and aged widows and
    widowers. Journal of Gerontology, 1975, 30, 225-
    229.

80. Heyman, D. K., & Gianturco, D. T. Long term adaptation by the elderly to bereavement. *Journal of Gerontology*, 1973, *28*, 359-362.

81. Bock, E. W., & Webber, I. L. Suicide among the elderly: Isolating widowhood and mitigating alternatives. *Journal of Marriage and the Family*, 1972, *34*, 24-31.

82. Kastenbaum, R. *Death, society and human experience.* St. Louis: Mosby, 1977.

DEATH EDUCATION
AND COUNSELING
FOR EVERYONE

The subject of death must be excluded from oblivion. It
is rightfully a part of each living day. We must read
and write and talk about it whenever the opportunity
naturally presents itself. Instead of being ignored, the
subject needs to be included in the daily ritual of living.

Agee and Ackerman
Why Children Must Mourn

INTRODUCTION

Any book dealing with the topic of sex differences must
address the question, "How much do these sex differences
really matter?" Teachers in the area of sex roles stress
again and again that while sex differences may be very
real, that is, have statistical significance and be able
to be replicated in many studies, the usual case is that
men and women are more alike than they are different.
Almost any characteristic you can think of is best depicted
using the concept of overlapping normal curves. For
example, while the literature reviewed in Chapter 3 tended
to show that females have higher death anxiety than do
males, it would be inaccurate to generalize those findings
to any one male or female. Utilizing the example of
death anxiety, Figure 6.1 depicts the usual condition
found in studying sex differences. You can see that females in this figure average higher death anxiety than do
males; however, the overlapping curve shows that many
males have higher death anxiety than many females. Con-
versely, many females have lower death anxiety than many
males. Caution in attempting to apply research findings
in the area of sex differences to any individual is
always justified.

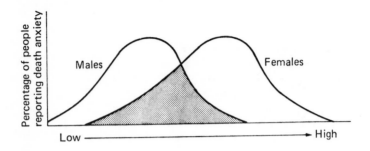

FIGURE 6.1. Model representation of sex differences in death anxiety.

This chapter will depart from the usual format of reviewing the literature on a specific topic in order to attempt
to address the question asked above, "How much do these
sex differences in death and death-related concerns
really matter?" Do they have meaning for the average
person, for the death educator, for the counselor of the
dying and/or the bereaved? As we attempt to answer these
questions, it will become clear that human beings, regardless of sex, share more in common than many people
may think. The human condition is a general one and it
supersedes even that most intimate identification of
individuals with their own gender. Therefore, while the
sex differences that we have examined in earlier chapters
are real ones and reflect the state of our culture today
in the area of death and death-related concerns, they
are not necessarily bases on which to build separate
death education or counseling programs. However, bearing
in mind the sex role stereotypes discussed in Chapter 2
which may be affecting our students and clients, we may
be able to strengthen specifics of our teaching and
counseling. This chapter is directed toward people in
the human service professions (education, social work,
counseling, nursing, psychology, etc.) who find themselves
dealing everyday with men and women who have death-
related concerns. It is likely that both males and
females stand in need of death education and counseling
at some time in their lives. Only when socialization
pressures have exerted influences toward denial, dependency, or stoicism is it necessary to be aware of and
address sex differences in death education and counseling.

REVIEWING THE FACTS

Before discussing death education and counseling for the
professional, it would perhaps be instructive to summarize
once again the areas of sex differences in death and

death-related concerns with which death educators and
counselors must be prepared to deal. The first area, of
course, is that of longevity itself. Women can expect
to live approximately eight years longer than men.
Implications of this statistic to the lives of people of
both sexes are staggering and frequently overlooked.
Although there are many complexities involved in attempting to understand why this statistic exists, practi-
cally this sex difference means that women can expect to
spend the last years of their lives on their own more
frequently than can men. Since these years often coincide
with the years of physical failing, women may be twice
hampered in trying to live independently without their
spouses at a time when it is becoming increasingly difficult to cope. Their early socialization toward dependency
and passivity may add to their physical failing to reduce
life satisfaction during the final decade of life.
Solutions to this problem are not easily found but, as
with many problems, the best approach may be to attempt
to prevent at least the most dramatic forms of the
problem by socializing females toward independence and
active assertiveness at an early age so that attitudinally
they will be more capable of coping independently when
left alone during that last decade. For men, this
statistic raises a whole set of questions, which again
are best addressed during youth rather than old age.
Such questions include: What is the relationship of
stress-related diseases to the stereotyped macho man?
What role do habits such as smoking, drinking, and lack
of exercise play in reinforcing the differential statistic? What life-style best ensures realization of genetic
longevity potential? Does expressiveness in emotional
life play a part in longevity? Given the facts concerning
sex differential in longevity, males may choose to examine
their traditional sex role socialization in a more serious
and highly motivated manner, secure in the knowledge that
there may well be "something for them" in changing some
aspects of the role which the male has traditionally
played in our culture and that this something may be
additional years of useful life.

In addition to the statistics on longevity itself,
apparent sex differences in death anxiety should be
familiar to interested human service professionals. Death
anxiety, or at least the admission of death anxiety,
seems to be higher for females than for males across the
life span. For educators and counselors this may mean
that women will be more approachable on these topics.
More women may elect courses in death and dying and more
women may present themselves for counseling either in an
attempt to cope with their anxieties or to handle their
losses. Once again, knowledgeable counselors and teachers
will need to be able to cope with males socialized not
to reveal emotions and with females who, while able to
admit their feelings, may have been socialized to depend

on others to help them achieve their goals, rather than assertively taking responsibility for their own growth.

Sex differences in suicide and homicide reveal to the human service professional that males may need more help in handling aggressive tendencies in positive ways. Learning to cope positively with aggression at a young age might have payoffs in many areas. It might reduce the adolescent male suicide statistics, the battered wife and child statistics, the male predominance in murder, and the male predominance in suicide. Therefore, any good death education or preventive counseling program should include material covering healthy coping techniques. Such material might help women to develop positive coping skills and reduce the excess number of their suicide attempts since they might not be as overwhelmed by feelings of anxiety, depression, and lack of control.

Finally, death educators and counselors need to be aware of the sex differences in handling bereavement and grief which are suggested by the research. Understanding of the role of support systems, and the increased risk of death to men of certain ages during bereavement, might well lead counselors to develop more widespread group approaches to loss in which the atmosphere is conducive to expression of feelings. Death educators might stress in their classes that grief is an almost universal phenomenon which will occur to all in their classes if they live long enough but that grief does not have to be handled alone, thus setting in motion attitudes which may allow their students to participate in support groups at a later date if necessary, regardless of socialization toward stoicism or emotional denial.

WHY PROFESSIONALS SHOULD BE DEATH EDUCATORS

Let's be clear on a basic premise. There can be no question as to whether death education should occur in our society. As is true of the issue of sex education, death education is occurring and will occur, regardless of our desires. Even if we clearly show that the knowledge of death is harmful for children under a certain age (which most death educators do not believe) there would be no way to keep the knowledge of death from them. Therefore, the question is not, "Should there be death education in our culture?", but rather, "What kind of death education does our society want?"

Who are the death educators in our society today? The main one, of course, is television. Nature abhors a vacuum. Since no one has been taking the lead in death education in the recent past, television has rushed in to fill the vacuum. This is true for all ages, although perhaps it has its greatest influence on the young, who have relatively little real personal experience with death to moderate their television impressions.

We have written elsewhere (1) about the peculiar impressions concerning death that children get from television. Suffice it to say here that children whose total view of death is based on television knowledge will have a hard time realizing the irreversibility of death. (The coyote on the roadrunner show is indestructible.) They will also have trouble realizing the finality of death. (A character on a soap opera dies but appears on another soap opera the following week.) In addition, they will not be prepared for the ongoing pain involved in the grieving process. (When characters die on a soap opera, they may be completely forgotten even by their closest relatives within a matter of weeks. Later shows may even revise the story line so that it will seem that the character whose wretched demise the children watched never really existed.)

TV news, of course, shows real death. John F. Kennedy, Lee Harvey Oswald, Martin Luther King, Robert Kennedy, Anwar Sadat, nameless soldiers and numerous shopkeepers and automobile drivers are shown in our homes in living color experiencing death. And then TV directors cut to a commercial and go on to other things. This kind of death education can be worse than none at all, as it doesn't allow time for processing of events. If viewers don't take time to talk about feelings, attitudes, and fears it is possible that this type of coverage will lead them to even greater levels of personal denial of death and/or to devaluation of human life.

The church and home together have historically handled death education. However, in recent years both of these institutions have deemphasized teaching about death. Churches often still handle aspects of death; the funeral service, for example, and the custom of providing food for the family offer immediate support for the bereaved. But this is after-the-fact handling. Few churches seem to have a logical, well-planned, sequential program of death education for their members. As for parents, many find the subject of death personally distasteful and are at a loss as to what to teach their children and when to teach it. Some even feel they are protecting their children by not discussing death and that this protection is a positive part of good parenting. The idea of protection is questionable in a society where one of every 20 children will lose a parent by death during childhood. But, as we've seen, fragmented and confusing information rushes in to fill the void left by parental refusal or inability to address the topic of death.

Schools have discovered death education in the past few
years. However, programs have generally consisted of
"hit or miss" type units or one course during secondary
school. One description of a three-day unit on death
education for fifth graders appeared in the Phi Delta
Kappan in 1978 and was criticized in the same issue (2,
3). For three days the children experienced the topic
of death in all subjects: reading, spelling, writing,
even math (they measured the dimensions for their own
coffins). The critique pointed out potential psychological
dangers of this approach. However, it stands today as a
good example of our current approach to the topic of
death education. As a society, we tend to ignore the
subject most of the time. Then we hold our breaths and
immerse students in the subject much as we rinse pets in
bad-smelling flea baths "for their own good"; then we
drop the topic and go back to "real life" subjects again.
Such educational approaches may tend to decrease, rather
than increase, acceptance of death as a part of normal
mainstream topics to be studied.

Colleges and universities frequently offer one or more
courses in death and dying, but generally no one is
required to take them. Therefore, we are still producing
large numbers of college-educated people, many of whom
are going to be working in human services, who have
little or no preparation for dealing with these universal
human truths: that death is an inevitable part of life
and that bereavement is a painful process, often necessi-
tating support for helping professionals.

In 1976, Dickinson published an article on the subject
of death education for physicians (4). He queried 113
medical schools concerning the type and amount of death
education offered to prospective doctors. His results
showed that only seven of the 107 (6.5 percent) responding
medical schools offered a full-term course on the subject
of death and dying. Of the remaining respondents, 44
(41 percent) stated that they had a mini-course and 42
(39 percent) stated that they had a "lecture or two" on
the subject. Fourteen (13.0 percent) reported no formal
death education course. Furthermore, of those who had
some kind of education, 73 percent had had such programs
for five years or less. Only 5 percent had included
death education in their curriculum for 10 years or more.
It is clear that even those professionals who will have
the most intimate and frequent contact with death are not
being exposed to death education on a regular basis.

Another form which death education is taking is that of
short workshops offered to the general public, and often
as in-service training for professionals who did not
receive such training as part of their regular education.
The quality of these programs differs greatly. However,
they almost universally share one thing in common. They

are too short and too intense to provide more than a beginning step in the necessary ongoing process of death education. In addition, there generally is little follow-up concerning their effect on participants, so their overall effectiveness cannot be evaluated.

One interesting attempt at death education was conducted by Robert Fulton via national newspapers. The course material was read by an estimated 15,000 people. Once again, it was difficult to assess the effect of such a presentation. However, the mere fact that so many news-papers cooperated to bring the course to so many people seems to underline both the current need for death edu-cation and society's new readiness to accept it.

In summary, because death is a fact of life, we need to be educated concerning it. Because we as a society in the recent past have become so distanced from death, we need responsible education concerning it. Finally, because information about death is coming to most of us only in disconnected and often unrealistic bits and pieces, we need a coherent framework of death education.

DEATH EDUCATION

Each of the topics involving sex differences in death and death-related concerns has applications for both educators and counselors. Indeed, death education and counseling concerning death-related matters have much in common. One way of viewing death education is as a pre-ventive mental health measure. To the extent that death education prepares students to face their own feelings about death, to accept the inevitability of death and loss and to anticipate and develop healthy coping behaviors, it can be regarded as preventive mental health care.

In any death education program, professionals must bear in mind certain principles if they are to be effective. Table 6.1 lists nine principles of death education which are intended to serve as a checklist of minimal qualifi-cations for helping professionals wishing to serve as death educators.

The first principle deals with knowledge of the cognitive stage of the learner. Ever since Piaget's pioneering work in stages of cognition became well known, educators have attempted to aim their teaching at the cognitive level of the child. We saw in Chapter 3 that research into the concept of death indicates that children pass through age-related stages of partial understanding on their way to mature understanding of the finality, universality, inevitability, irreversibility, and personal nature of death. Piaget's early research indi-

TABLE 6.1   Principles of Death Education

Teacher Possesses:

Knowledge of cognitive stage of learner
Knowledge of subject matter
Willingness to address only expressed concerns of learner
Willingness to listen as well as talk
Encouragement of learner's natural curiosity
Natural involvement of children in funerals and memorial
   services
Open honesty in discussing death related material
Willingness to share own feelings as well as knowledge
   when a death has occurred
Encouragement of consideration of death in building
   philosophy of life (adult students)

---

cated that there were few if any sex differences in
young children's cognitive understanding. The research
into the understanding of death in like manner failed to
show sex differences at least until around age 11 or 12,
when boys begin to deny thinking about death and to deny
fear and anxiety more than do girls. This sex difference
probably has to do less with cognition than with affect.
By this age boys have probably learned that to appear
masculine, they must seem to be "cool" and unperturbed
on every topic. Therefore, death educators working with
adolescents or adults may have to remember to expend
extra effort in structuring the course so that males as
well as females understand that expressiveness is permitted
and rewarded. Educators may also have to spend more time
with males than with females if they wish to establish
an atmosphere of open communication in the course.

The second principle for the death educator is knowledge
of subject matter. There is a large and ever-growing
body of material available in the field of death education.
Such topics as cross-cultural rituals surrounding death,
psychological meaning of funeral customs, the legal
definition of death, euthanasia, suicide, longevity
statistics, causes of death, attitudes and fears of
death, typical grief reactions, methods of increasing
longevity, etc. form the core of most classes on death
education. The premise of this book is that it is also
important to be aware of sex differences which exist in
the field and to acquaint your students with them so as
to enhance their ability to plan for their individual
futures.

The third principle, willingness to address only expressed
concerns of the learner, is one which applies mostly to

younger children. Death education shares much in common
with sex education in that both are highly emotional
topics which parents and other educators may have problems
discussing in a natural manner. There's an old sex
education story about a 6-year-old who asked his mother
about the newborn baby next door. His question was,
"Mommy, where did Mrs. Jones get her baby?" Twenty
minutes later, after the anxious mother had dutifully
given a detailed description of fertilization, pregnancy,
and the three stages of labor, the glassy-eyed 6-year-old
said, "But Mommy, all I wanted to know was, what hospital
Mrs. Jones and the baby were in." Taking a cue from sex
education, a basic principle of death education with
children, then, is to listen to the question asked;
answer it; and then wait to see if further questions are
forthcoming. In certain situations, as children grow up
and learn to inhibit their curiosity, parents and teachers
may have to probe for feelings, especially anxiety or
fear, which may lie behind a child's question. Once again,
girls may more readily admit fears and ask questions,
especially after around age 10 or 11, because of differential socialization.

The fourth principle is one which holds true at every
age. It is to do at least as much listening as talking
if death education is being carried out individually or
with a small group. With large groups, more didactic
teaching and less interaction is the rule. With small
groups, however, listening not only enables the educator
to pinpoint the developmental stage and readiness of the
student, it also helps to create a relaxed atmosphere
that serves to invite further discussion and shows
respect for students' views. Once again this principle
permits reinforcement of open honesty on the part of
males as well as females as they share fears, anxieties,
and knowledge.

A fifth principle of death education is encouragement of
the learner's natural curiosity. Somehow within the
recent past our society has taught children as well as
adults that death is not a topic to be addressed via the
usual means. Authority figures in the home or the school
have not tended to discuss it. Utilization of the
natural curiosity of children as well as adults will
enable the alert death educator to find many entrees for
discussing death in a natural and appropriate manner.
Everyday occurrences such as changing seasons and death
of pets may allow boys and girls as well as men and women
to confront the topic of death with a willing educator.

A seventh principle which death educators need to bear
in mind is the willingness to share their own feelings
as well as their knowledge concerning death. While this
principle may not be absolutely essential in all cases,
it does create a model that encourages the students to

be open about their feelings. In addition, if the death
educator is a father, expression of his emotions may
encourage the boy child to feel free to express his own.
In contrast, keeping a "stiff upper lip" in the face of
a loss may be misinterpreted as evidence that the father
really didn't love the deceased or that he doesn't care
that the person is dead. In any case, death educators
once again need to be reminded of the socialized sex
differences in allowing oneself to express emotional
experiences, and perhaps need to encourage boys more
than girls at adolescence or beyond to express themselves
fully.

The final general principle is one of encouragement of
consideration of the reality of death in building a
philosophy of life. This principle applies most directly
to adolescents and adults, and may be viewed as a key
to promoting good mental health throughout life. Thinking
adolescents and adults frequently recognize existential
factors which affect their interpretation of what gives
meaning to life. One of the leading authorities in
group psychotherapy has suggested that there are five
existential factors which people must address if they
are to develop good mental health (5). Death education
programs, whether done in the home or in school, lend
themselves to addressing these concerns. They are:

1. Recognizing that life is at times unfair and unjust;
    a realization encountered time and time again in
    death education, but perhaps nowhere as clearly as
    in the examination of male-female differential
    longevity rates.
2. Recognizing that ultimately there is no escape from
    some of life's pain and from death. This recognition,
    promoted by the entire subject matter of death edu-
    cation, may promote acceptance or at least facilitate
    awareness of the inevitability of pain and loss.
    Such awareness and acceptance may lead to the develop-
    ment of more positive coping skills.
3. Recognizing that no matter how close I get to other
    people, I still face life alone. This recognition,
    promoted by longevity statistics as well as by
    research on widowhood, may be more helpful to females
    than to males as females are more likely to be
    widowed. However, recognition by both sexes of the
    essential aloneness of the human condition may cause
    both sexes to develop characteristics of strength,
    independence, and the prizing of honest human relation-
    ships.
4. Facing the basic issues of my life and thus living my
    life more honestly and being less caught up in
    trivialities. If death education does any one thing,
    it helps us to put day-to-day living in perspective;
    to take time to smell the roses and not to become
    hysterical about burning the peas. Death education

can be the ultimate in values clarification. It
forces consideration of quality of life as well as
quantity of life issues and hopefully encourages
perspectives on such things as smoking, exercise,
diet, alcohol consumption, life-style, etc. This
data may be more important to males than to females
as consideration of it may result in wiser life
choices, thus reducing the sex differential in
longevity.

5. Learning that I must take ultimate resonsibility for
the way I live my life, no matter how much guidance
and support I get from others. The nature of death
education with its empahsis on transience and on
personal meaning also brings up, sometimes for the
first time, the fact that responsibility for one's
own growth in life cannot be avoided or left to someone else and that lack of growth cannot be blamed
on anyone else. Thus, death education can promote
an individual's search for meaning in his/her
existence.

COUNSELING THE BEREAVED

While death education has been viewed by some as helping
to prepare people to face the reality of bereavement
more realistically, it cannot eliminate the need for
bereavement counseling. Our society is currently lacking
the organized resources to cope with grief and bereavement which were built into a simpler, more rural past
where extended families and strong church ties were the
rule rather than the exception. Therefore, human service
workers from fields including education, counseling,
social work, psychology, and nursing may be called on to
help develop new systems for providing support throughout
the grief process.

Such support begins, of course, with a minimal understanding of the effect of death and grief on individuals,
such as that presented in Chapter 5. In addition, human
service workers must be able to describe what is meant
by the process of "working through grief."

Spiegel (6) described the normal grief process as consisting of a series of tasks which the bereaved must
perform in order to emerge from grief with energy to
invest in new relationships and activities. These tasks,
taken together, provide a good insight into the mechanics
of grief work.

Spiegel referred to the first task as the release of
grief. In his view, it involves both initial acceptance
of the death and the ability to let go emotionally and
express pain and sorrow. This first step may be harder
for males than for females because of their socialization

toward stoicism and emotional inexpressiveness. In
addition to feeling that they have to be strong for
others, many males may actually fear that if they let go
emotionally they may not be able to regain control; that
they may be overwhelmed by grief and unable to handle it.
While some females may also share this fear, it generally
is not as powerful a threat to a female's total identity
as it is to that of a male, who may have internalized
independence and competence as the core of his identity.
To be overwhelmed by emotion may be to feel "unmanned"
and therefore less than competent. Males may need more
reassurance that they will receive support and that,
although painful, expression of emotion is healthy and
will end.

The second process in working through grief, according
to Spiegel, is structuring. The chaotic emotions which
death has stirred up; the fears, the love-hate ambivalence,
the anger, guilt, and resentment, may threaten to over-
whelm people if they are not able to begin to organize
them into some kind of framework for examination. Spiegel
suggests that such structuring might start with clarifying
the relationship with the deceased, a process which
generally involves intense preoccupation with the memory
of the deceased, at least for a short period of time.

The third process in grief work is the continued redis-
covery of the fact of death, leading to final acceptance.
Spiegel suggests that such final acceptance comes only
after a period of time during which the bereaved verifies
the loss by talking with other people and by revisiting
places shared with the deceased.

The fourth process in grief work is an existential one
which Spiegel calls the decision for life. The bereaved
must make a decision, often with the support of loved
ones or helping professionals, that life is worth living
in spite of the loss she or he has suffered.

The fifth process of grief work, and an important one to
anyone who would counsel bereaved persons, is the
expression of unacceptable emotions and desires. If not
expressed, these emotions are frequently repressed and
through a process known as conversion reaction (the
changing of an unacceptable feeling into its opposite)
become central in an unrealistic glorification of the
deceased. Such a glorification differs from normal
memorialization in that it admits no flaw in the deceased,
thus creating a perfect individual in comparison to whom
no living individual seems interesting and no activity
which cannot be shared with the lost paragon seems worth-
while. Alternatively, if negative emotions and desires
concerning the deceased are not expressed, bereaved
persons may turn these negative emotions against themselves, becoming embedded in a web of guilt and self-

hatred. Such handling of negative feelings obviously
poses a serious threat to the completion of grief work,
threatening to halt the grief process prematurely. Once
again, the counselor should bear in mind that men frequently require more support and permission to express
negative as well as positive feelings about the deceased.

The sixth step described by Spiegel in the process of
grief work is evaluation of the loss. Here again, outside caregivers may assist in helping the bereaved to
judge as realistically as possible the extent of the loss
and the possibility of creative substitution for that
loss. When death occurs, bereaved persons frequently
feel that their loss is complete and ignore positive
aspects of their life which still remain. In this phase,
women may more frequently need help than men. Traditionally, more of a woman's identity is dependent upon her
status as a wife and/or mother; that is, women may have
a greater tendency to define themselves in terms of
their relationships than do men. If this is true, loss
of a key relationship might be more overwhelming to a
woman than to a man and more difficult to put in realistic
perspective.

The seventh step described by Spiegel is called incorpora-
tion of the deceased. It refers to the ability of the
bereaved to acquire a realistic insight of the merits
and weaknesses of the dead person and to integrate such
a realistic picture into an accurate memory. This frequently requires the bereaved not only to work through
the negative emotions toward the deceased described
above, but also to find a way to forgive the deceased
for real and/or imagined wrongs committed during their
lifetimes.

The final step in grief work, according to Spiegel, is
making a commitment to a new way of life without the
deceased. Spiegel calls this the chance of a new
orientation. Even in the most painful loss, elements
of new freedom and independence can be found. Women,
perhaps more often than men, must be helped to give
themselves permission to experience and enjoy this new
freedom and independence without guilt or anxiety.
Especially, dependent females must be helped to take
the initiative in finding meaning in loss. As the
Nichols (7) have suggested, "In death and in grief we
do not need as much protection from painful experiences
as we need the boldness to face them.... What a blessing
to take the time to integrate loss into our lives so
that when a love is lost, our capacity to love is not
lost also. From our grief can come growth" (7, p. 96).

The central goal of grief counseling is to maximize this
potential for growth and to aid individuals in passing
through the grief process to reach the point where they

can remember without excess pain, can experience an
increase in energy, and can feel free to invest that
energy in new relationships and experiences. Grief
counseling is always difficult since bereavement entails
powerful emotions which may make some counselors uncomfortable. In addition, grief counseling is often
threatening to counselors because the bereaved person
may evoke in the counselor the awareness of the very
real probability that the counselor will experience
bereavement in his or her own life.

Corazzini (8) has suggested that there are four major
tasks of the counselor. They include (a) remaining open
to the loss of the other and resisting blocking or dis-
counting the process; (b) developing empathy with the
bereaved which permits the counselor to experience the
complex feelings of the bereaved and to communicate
understanding of the experience to the client; (c) encouraging reminiscing, which seems essential to moving
through the grief process; and (4) insisting on the
loss by reminding the mourner that the death has really
occurred, especially in the first few days of bereavement.
Other aims of grief counseling have been summarized by
Raphael in an excellent chapter which describes a
psychiatric model of bereavement counseling (9). She
spells out four principal aims: to offer basic human
comfort and support, to encourage the expression of
grief, to promote the mourning process, and to supplement
the personal support system which already exists in
order to facilitate the process of grief.

Raphael also presents a therapeutic assessment interview
format which she believes is helpful in bereavement
counseling once the initial phase of shock, disbelief,
and denial is over. Her format includes exploration of
the circumstances around the death itself, discussion of
the unique relationship which the bereaved had with the
deceased and the loss of meaning which the death brings
with it, and examination of the total response of the
bereaved to the death including such elements as feelings,
coping responses, support systems, and financial problems.
She suggests certain circumstances which might require
further evaluation and intensified counseling because of
the special problems inherent in them. These include
deaths by suicide, deaths in major accidents, deaths of
children, multiple bereavements occurring simultaneously,
unresolved grief as of the childhood loss of a parent,
and deaths in which a single elderly person loses a
parent for whom he or she has been responsible.

TOWARD A MODEL OF BEREAVEMENT COUNSELING

In developing a model for bereavement counseling, both
the tasks of the counselor as identified by Corazzini

and the tasks of the bereaved, as identified by Raphael, are important to keep in mind. It is also important, however, to remember that grief is a process and that because it tends to follow a sequential pattern, certain techniques may be helpful at one time which may not be helpful at another time.

Herzog has suggested a three-phase model of bereavement. He envisioned bereaved people as passing through the stages of resuscitation, recovery, and renewal (10). Although his work was based on bereavement following suicide cases, these terms seem applicable to grief reactions in general. Basically, Herzog believed that the resuscitation stage only lasted for the first 24 hours after the death, the rehabilitation stage lasted for the first six months after death, and the renewal stage lasted from six months to approximately one year after death. These times seem somewhat short when one considers that grief may last up to two years after the death. Nevertheless, if we accept the phases, match them with client tasks and counselor tasks derived from a variety of sources, the following suggestive model of grief counseling begins to emerge.

It is not the intent of the model to suggest that all bereaved persons need counseling. Many people experiencing a death will have the inner resources and the external support to work through the grief process without any type of professional intervention. However, in our increasingly mobile and fragmented society, many more people may need professional help than was true in the past.

Women, in particular, may need access to bereavement counseling more in the future, as they are having smaller families and are outliving their spouses. In addition, as we have pointed out before, at least until very recently, women have not been socialized to lead independent, assertive life-styles. Therefore, external support may be welcomed by a growing number of women who are attempting to deal with loss and bereavement issues.

Men, on the other hand, as we have seen, may need special help in the early stages of grief. Facing loss head on without attempting escape by drugs or alcohol and ventilating feelings are difficult tasks. Traditional males may be more reluctant to take this first step, especially with family and friends with whom they've always fulfilled the strong, unemotional male role. In light of the higher incidence in mortality among widowers, it would seem especially important to recognize the potential roadblock to expression of feelings early in the counseling process.

TABLE 6.2 A Model for Counseling the Bereaved

Phase	Duration	Task of Bereaved	Dangers to Bereaved	Task of Counselor	Personal and Professional Dangers to Counselor
Resuscitation	First 24 hours after death (May last up to 2 weeks)	Ventilation of disbelief, shock, anger, loss	May attempt to avoid grief by tranquilization, alcohol, or other drugs	Listening Being there	Being overwhelmed by emotions Feeling awkward
		Initial acceptance	May be overwhelmed by people and events	Accepting feelings	Feeling for, instead of with
				Helping person to accept real- ity of death	Aiding denial rather than acceptance
Rehabilitation	First six months after death	Continuing growth in acceptance of death	May continue denial	Educating about normal aspects of grief, e.g., nutrition, physical symptoms	May underrate the impact of the loss
		Evaluation of the extent of loss and the meaning of the loss	May make pre- cipitous life changes		May overlook complexity of relationships
			May repress powerful nega- tive emotions	Warn about problems that may ensue	May terminate counseling pre- maturely

156

Rehabilitation (Continued)	Gradual expression of negative as well as positive emotions and desires regarding the deceased	May deny life, become depressed, "drop out"	Consulting with each family member	May fail to structure fully enough
			Continuing to promote acceptance of death	
	Making a decision for life		Structuring evaluation of the extent of loss and change on life	
			Encouraging the working through of unfinished feelings toward the deceased; the bad as well as the good	

TABLE 6.2 A Model for Counseling the Bereaved (Cont'd)

Phase	Duration	Task of Bereaved	Dangers to Bereaved	Task of Counselor	Personal and Professional Dangers to Counselor
Rehabilitation (Continued)				Aiding in the planning for the future	
				Continuing support and comfort giving	
				Confronting gently concerning unfinished grief work.	
Renewal	Six months to one year After death (may last up to 18 months)	Healthy memorialization Making a new commitment to life; new friends, new activities	May idealize deceased May increase distance between self and others	Further exploring of alternatives Encouraging a commitment to a new way of life	May encourage continued dependency on counseling relationship

Renewal (Continued)	Increased vulnerability to psycho- physiological disease	Supporting de- cisions that affirm life
		Recognizing the growth and re- inforcing new strengths discovered
		Terminating counseling

In order to be of most help to a grieving person, human service workers need to prepare themselves for working with the bereaved. Such preparation involves as a minimum the following five guidelines:

1. Be clear about your view of death. Work through your feelings on such questions as: What fears do you have when you think about death? Does the presence of death threaten you? Embarrass you? Make you feel impotent? What meaning does death bring to life in your opinion?

2. Be clear about how you view one who is bereaved. Here, as in most counseling situations, feeling with (empathy) is much more important than feeling for (sympathy).

3. Be willing to reach out to the bereaved. In our modern culture, these people are often avoided or ignored once the initial response to the death is over. Widows especially are often instructed to deny problems and act brave, cheerful, and in control. This may block their initiative in seeking out helping professionals.

4. Be aware that the normal grieving process can last over a year and that anniversary reactions are likely to occur on special dates throughout the first two years after the death (e.g., wedding anniversaries, birthdays, and the anniversary of the death).

5. Be aware that the goal of grief therapy is to aid the individual in passing through one of life's most stressful situations to a position of reinvestment in life. Each individual reacts in different ways to the stress of death, making sensitivity to individual differences absolutely essential.

SUMMARY

The purpose of this chapter was to examine the implications which sex differences in death and death-related concerns should have on the death educator and counselor. Death education is not only a legitimate topic of study; it also can be viewed as preventive mental health care in that it can help people to see death as an intimate, inevitable, and not necessarily totally negative component of life. In this way death education and counseling share much in common.

Principles of death education that addressed both age and sex as necessary were suggested. The elements of grief therapy were explored, and a suggested model was proposed for therapeutic intervention based on the sequence which grief seems to take and the tasks involved for both the bereaved and the counselor. Dangers to both the counselor and the bereaved were suggested in each phase of the sequence. Finally, general guidelines for helping professionals dealing with death, grief, and loss were reviewed

REFERENCES

1. Stillion, J. M., & Wass, H.   Children and death.
    In H. Wass (Ed.), Dying: facing the facts.   Washing-
    ton: Hemisphere, 1979.

2. Mueller, J. M.   I taught about death and dying, Phi
    Delta Kappan, 1978, 79, 60, 117.

3. Freeman, J.   Death and dying in three days?   Phi
    Delta Kappan, 1978, 79, 60, 118.

4. Dickinson, G.   Death education in U.S. medical
    schools.   Journal of Medical Education, 1976, 51,
    134-136.

5. Yalom, I.   The theory and practice of group psycho-
    therapy.   New York: Basic Books, 1975.

6. Spiegel, V.   The grief process: Analysis and counsel-
    ing.   Nashville, Tenn.: Abington, 1973.

7. Nichols, R., & Nichols, J.   A time for grief and
    growth.   In E. Kübler-Ross, Death: The final stage
    of growth.   Englewood Cliffs, N.J.: Prentice-Hall,
    1975.

8. Corazzini, J. G.   The theory and practice of loss
    therapy.   In B. M. Schoenberg (Ed.), Bereavement
    counseling: A multidisciplinary handbook.   Westport,
    Conn.: Greenwood, 1980.

9. Raphael, B.   A psychiatric model for bereavement
    counseling.   In B. M. Schoenberg (Ed.), Bereavement
    counseling: A multidisciplinary handbook.   Westport,
    Conn.: Greenwood, 1980.

10. Herzog, A.   A clinical study of parental response
    to adolescent death by suicide with recommendations
    for approaching the survivors.   In N. L. Faberow
    (Ed.), Proceedings of the fourth international
    conference for suicide prevention.   Los Angeles,
    Calif.: Delmar, 1968.

INDEX